Praise for Note to Self

With little knowledge of the monastic life, I had never heard of a Rule of Life. But I started to cry reading the first few pages of LaFond's book because it felt like it was written for me. As a confirmed workaholic and desperate to find some balance in my life, I now believe if I follow the book's spiritual prescription, I may finally be saved and learn to enjoy the rest of my life in a more fulfilling way.

Sean Tracey
Director of *The Jesus Guy* documentary

As America's religious landscape changes rapidly, Charles LaFond offers a compelling invitation to unbundle one of Christianity's great gifts and write our own Rule of Life. With humor, vulnerability, and rigor, LaFond illustrates how we can coach ourselves into better habits and mindsets following the ancient monastic practice. Inspiring and practical!

—Casper ter Kuile
Ministry Innovation Fellow
Harvard Divinity School

LaFond effortlessly transitions between anecdote and teaching, history and reflection. By opening himself to us in Note to Self, *he allows us all to learn from his monastic experiences and beyond. This thorough but gentle guide to writing our own Rule of Life is useful to everyone: Christians, Jews, atheists. Everyone. I'm excited to get started.*

—Saul Aryeh Kohn

Opening this book is like sitting next to a beloved uncle who has been around the world many times; who loves you enough to ask questions that break open your heart. Charles intersperses profound wisdom with stories that amaze and delight. By the end of the book, you will know not only who he is but also more than you imagined possible about who you are.

—Carolyn Metzler
Episcopal priest and spiritual director

As a remedy to the overcommitted, harried, and largely unconscious life, Charles LaFond offers this beautiful book. Blending ancient monastic wisdom with the unique needs of our time, he helps guide us in gaining true freedom in our lives...If you have ever felt adrift in your life, ever felt the anxiety of not knowing how your deep values might best come to expression in your daily living, you must read this book!

—James H. Reho
Author of *Tantric Jesus:*
The Erotic Heart of Early Christianity

Until I read this book, I had never considered writing my own book of life—my own Rule based on what I know in my heart of hearts I need to stay close to God and balanced in life. Charles's honesty about his journey inspired me to see my own journey as worthwhile and important. Thank you, Charles, for awakening what is good and right in our heart of hearts.

—Nancy Malloy
Episcopal priest
St. Laurence, Colorado

NOTE TO SELF

© 2018 Forward Movement

All rights reserved.

ISBN: 9790880284479

Printed in USA

inspire disciples. empower evangelists.

NOTE TO SELF

*Creating Your Guide
to a More Spiritual Life*

Charles LaFond

Foreword by John Philip Newell

Forward Movement
Cincinnati, Ohio

Dedication

To the many people
on the many retreats
who, on hearing about
a Rule of Life,
said,
I want one!
Teach me how to write one!
Write that book!

And to my black Lab, Kai,
who never left my side
and who reminds me always
to use my Rule to be my best self.

Table of Contents

Foreword

Note to Self: Creating Your Guide to a More Spiritual Life is an important book. And it belongs urgently to this moment in time.

Western Christianity, as we have known it, is in a state of collapse. Some try to deny this. Others acknowledge that we're in trouble but act as if what we need is more of the same, with a bit of new window dressing. And then there are others, like Charles LaFond, who see that what we are being called into is a new birthing.

What is trying to be born within us or, I would prefer to say, born again within us is a wisdom that our Christian household knew in its earliest centuries but forgot when we got into bed with the Roman Empire in the fourth century. We bought the lie of hierarchical power that truth is to be dispensed from above rather than mined from within. We began to think that spiritual truth, such as a Rule of Life, needed to be dictated to us by those in charge. We forgot the vital teaching of Jesus that the kingdom of God is within us. The wisdom of God, the light of God, the consciousness of God is at the heart of our being. It is pure gift, and it is longing to come forth again.

One of the earliest teachers in Celtic Christianity was once asked for a Rule of Life by a young woman. He replied to her that she shouldn't ask him. Rather, she should learn to read what God had written into her heart. And once she had learned to read what was etched into her soul, then she should write it out on a piece of paper and allow that to be her Rule of Life. But, he said, and this is the big "but" of the story, once she had written out on a piece of paper what she had read in her heart, then she was to compare what she had written with the wisdom of Jesus. If there was discord between what she read in her own soul and what she heard in Jesus, then she was to know that she had misread her heart. If this was the case, she needed to go back and read her heart again.

These words are critically important for us to hear. And they are like the words written in this fine book by Charles LaFond. We all need to do our own reading of the soul. No one else can do this work for us. We each need to keep reading a Rule of life and love that has been written uniquely onto each of our souls.

We are fortunate to have Charles LaFond among us. He is a beautiful son of our Christian household. And he is helping us remember a spiritual practice that will be part of our rebirthing.

John Philip Newell
Author, *Listening for the Heartbeat of God: A Celtic Spirituality*
Edinburgh, Scotland

Preface

We humans need reminders.

That is what happens in church. We listen to passages from scripture and to words that describe the Last Supper. We listen over and over and over again. But then Sunday afternoon happens, and Sunday night. And by Monday, we have forgotten. And yet…

Would we work on our issues of sin and guilt without Lent? Would we imagine wonder without Epiphany? Would we spontaneously pledge in churches without a stewardship campaign? Would we consider the gifts of life without Easter? Perhaps. Fleetingly. Occasionally. Accidentally. Alone.

To remember how to live, we need constant reminders. In making an effort to be better people, we need help to choose kindness and goodness. We need a way to train our minds and souls to be good and kind and to make good choices in the same way that athletes train their bodies to have motor-memory, so that when the ball comes, their training kicks in and the body responds.

A Rule of Life is an ancient technology for building soul-memory, for training minds and souls to be kind and good. It is a technology of grace that we can offer to ourselves.

I am grateful to my editor Leonard Freeman whose patience, counsel, and challenge have formed a book from an idea and a Rule. I am thankful for the Episcopal clergy and bishop of the Diocese of Chicago who helped me consider this material in a clergy retreat. I am grateful also to Richelle Thompson whose wisdom has guided this process and to Scott Gunn whose shepherding of my early ideas for a series of books gave me the courage and determination to be a writer. Forward Movement publishes works that help move the spiritual life forward day by day by day. And a Rule of Life is just that—a movement day by day through the life we call spiritual.

It is my hope that you make good choices each day, choices that bring you and others peace and even some joy. My Rule of Life helps me to remember to make good choices. I hope yours will do that for you.

Charles LaFond
Christ the King Sunday
A turret in The Cathedral of Saint John's in the Wilderness
Denver, Colorado

PART I

WHY A RULE OF LIFE

Chapter 1

Introduction: A Rule of Life

Though I live in New Mexico, I have kept my home in Black Water Bluff, New Hampshire. It is a wooden 1847 farmhouse and pottery studio, warmed by three wood stoves and nestled in the foothills of New Hampshire's White Mountains. I often walk by the Blackwater River for which the old farm is named and hike into the hilly forests of New Hampshire's backwoods. I walk with my English black Lab Kai, whose name reminds me of the *kairos* love of God, of playfulness and community. Kai is familiar with each stump and smell along the way. And he will often plant, stopping to protect me from moose and coyote.

We walk an old logging trail. There are lots of trails to the left and right that lead who-knows-where but nowhere I want to go. If I take the wrong path, I will end up lost in the woods late at night. If I am listening to an audio book (and I usually am), I will often become so engrossed in the plot that my steps fall one after another without much consideration, until I feel a tug on the leash. Kai has stopped at the fork in the path, his head hung low, looking at me out of the tops of his eyes with a furrowed brow, telling me that a nearly imperceptible fork just happened along the path. Instead of staying on the main road that curves to the left, I have walked straight ahead and by doing so have put myself onto a side path that will take me to the wrong place at the foot of the wrong mountain. The result would be a very long walk home—or worse, a night lost in the woods. The longer I travel that unintended path, the farther I am from my intended destination.

Kai stops me from taking the wrong path, and we cut through the small brush to the correct trail. His tail wags madly at having done his good deed of the day for both of us.

I think life can be like that. Hopefully, we live life with some vision of the life-path we want to walk. But if we are not frequently checking our position and the map, we take wrong pathways and end up in unintended places, doing any number of unintended things. We are off track simply because we were not paying attention to the pathway we intended to take.

A Rule of Life is an ancient technology to help keep us on a right pathway. Developed and used by religious communities male and female the world over (Benedictines, Franciscans, etc.), a Rule of Life helps keep the monks and nuns on track in managing their lives and growing their souls. The purpose of this book is to encourage and help you to develop your own Rule of Life.

Rules

A Rule of Life can sound like a daunting thing. Indeed, it sounds practically unAmerican! Rules—even the word itself—can feel confining and imprisoning, conjuring images of frustrated, ancient nuns wielding rulers to rap our knuckles if we step out of line. Our society highly values open options and places a very low premium on commitment. Why work on a marriage when we can trade this wife or husband in for a newer, fresher, younger model? Why work on weight loss when I can buy bigger clothes? Sometimes circumstances demand a change. But so often we simply end up in places in life rather than consciously working toward them.

Making choices, determining a way forward in life, means grieving the loss of the choices not taken, the paths not chosen. Our society moves on to the next thing so fast that there is no time for grieving the way not traveled. Some of those un-chosen paths are very attractive and desirable. And those un-chosen and un-trod paths are not necessarily bad or wrong paths, though some might well lead to unhappiness and pain for us or others. But all too often, they are not the paths we were intended to walk.

For the past 1,300 years, we have moved away from the notion that humans are basically evil and streaked with good to an awareness that humans are basically good and streaked with evil. As our theology heals and grows, we need not let the pendulum swing too far in the other direction so that all things—all paths—are deemed good. Some things that are good for others and that might be enjoyable need to be left on the shelf. When we choose one thing—having done the hard work of discerning that such is the right and best thing to do— we must then acknowledge that we will need to let go of the many other choices we could have made.

A Rule of Life is simply a series of letters we write to ourselves to keep us on the path we want to take. A Rule reminds us of who we are and what we want. It is a technology for living that can be imported from monasteries and into our lives. While a Rule of Life is a simple tool, it has great promise. This book will explain the value of a Rule of Life, how to make one, and how to use a Rule over many decades of choice-making and discernment.

Note to Self

Sometimes I write a Post-it note or tape a piece of paper on the front door so that I do not leave the house without remembering something. *Remember to bring that book for tonight's meeting. Remember to spend time walking today on your lunch hour. Remember yoga at 5.* These little notes are helpful. These notes to myself are my way of remembering what I want in a world and life with many choices.

We need to make choices so that we may live. Sometimes our choices are good, healthy, wise choices, and at other times we make poor choices because of fatigue, inflamed ego, insecurity, greed, envy, a lust for some commodity, or an addiction-driven brain.

Eat the doughnut; you only live once!
  No! It is your fifth one today, and you are a diabetic!
Oh, go ahead, life is short.
  No, you will be short if they remove your feet because of infections from diabetes.
Oh, come on, it's just a doughnut...

But what if I read my page, my "note to self" (we call it a "chapter"), from my Rule of Life that describes my hopes for my life regarding food? What if the food or health page— one I wrote myself—were read that very day and it said that I committed to being careful about sugar and eating in moderation so that I could enjoy healthy food and a healthy body? What if I read that page as if it were one of those notes we put on the front door? *Remember: If you are offered sugar today, try to avoid it except in moderation because you are sensitive to sugars.*

What if the note on the door was a page that reminded me how I feel about kindness, nudging me to treat others gently and with compassion? Or a note I wrote to myself about getting enough rest—the importance of confining work to eight hours per day?

A Rule of Life is a fancy, ancient, and religious term for a simple collection of "notes to self" that you write and read back to yourself once a day as a reminder of how you want to live your life. It is like a manifesto or a set of guidelines. Simply put, you choose a dozen or two dozen or three dozen topics about your goals for these areas—then you write them down. Many people write thirty notes to self because that is about one each day for a month. At the end of the month you simply go back to page one and begin reading the statements again. In a year you read each page about twelve times. This way you never go for more than a month without being reminded of the top thirty things you think are important to your living a good life.

Once you have made your list of thirty key topics, write some notes for each one. Next, you expand each Rule into a page of self-coaching so that all you need to do is read one page a day in a cycle that matches the number of topics (pages) you have written. If you want to coach yourself on ten subjects (for example: money, rest, health, food, work, prayer, friendship, exercise, kindness, and play) then you write ten topics, expand each topic into a series of paragraphs about your hope for that subject in your life, and then you simply read the ten pages, one a day, for ten days, and repeat. A Rule of Life, then, is a set of reminders you write to yourself, for yourself, so that you reconnect your vision for your life with your actual daily life.

An Example of a Rule of Life

Let's take work as an example. Last week, I got up, brushed my teeth, did my praying and my listening. Then I read that day's chapter (one written page) from my Rule of Life. My Rule has a "chapter" (about a page) on many aspects of my life. Each day I read one, and then I turn the page to read a new one on the next day. When I get to the end, I start again.

So this one day I sat down to read my Rule of Life. I opened the three-ring binder that contains my Rule of Life and moved the red ribbon from Chapter 22 to the next page—Chapter 23. I noticed that the topic of Chapter 23 is work, and I read on. (Yesterday's chapter was on food, I note to myself with an awareness of the good choice I made to have salmon and green bean bake. Good job, chapter on food!!!) As I read my chapter on work, I remember (re-member...bring back together) my thoughts on work. As I read, I remember that I sometimes work too hard. I remember that I sometimes try to use work to build self-esteem, when in fact it never really can. I remember, as I read, that I want to work a reasonable amount, not an excessive one. My chapter on work reminds me that work takes up a lot of my week, so I might as well enjoy the work I do and choose my work carefully.

It takes about three minutes to read the page from my Rule of Life, and when I am done, I close the Rule of Life binder, change into my suit and drive off to work. When my colleague suggests that a letter I wrote needs to be rewritten, I remember my Rule chapter of the morning, and my self-esteem is not shaken. I smile. I rewrite it. No drama. No ego storm. I thank the person for the advice and do it. (And the coworker was right...it needed to be rewritten!) Then I get an invitation to an evening meeting. It would be my fourth night at work in one week so I gently, politely decline, saying that I would be glad to read the minutes of the meeting afterward but that, no, I am sorry that I will not to be able to attend the meeting. No drama. No shame. But also no giving in to pressure to attend.

A Rule of Life is your own tool to set your own boundaries with your own life. It reminds you about what you love and what you consider important. In short, it is a daily coaching by you, for you, on various aspects of your life. And it works wonders.

This book is about how to imagine a Rule of Life, how to design, write, live by, and edit a Rule of Life so that you have a series of stepping stones upon which to walk through an effective, contented life—inasmuch as you have control over your own choices.

Do bad things happen? Sure they do, and many of these situations are out of your control. But it makes sense to be reminded regularly of your own hopes for various aspects of your life, so that the things you do have control over are managed in ways that are most likely to bring you happiness and less likely to bring you suffering.

One choice at a time. One day at a time.

As an Episcopal priest, I have counseled hundreds of people who tell me about their lives—and sometimes about their poor choices. They tell me about how small the choices were, but that because there were so many of these wrong choices over a long period of time, they ended up on the wrong road, off of their life path. "How did I get to this place?" they ask.

I have listened to spouses weep as they tell me about the choices their partners have made. I have listened to clergy and office workers recount with crystalline clarity how they watched their CEO, manager, chairman of the board, dean, rector, canon, or bishop make one tiny, poor choice after another—dragging the people who work under them into a maelstrom of grief and loss.

There is so much suffering being visited upon people, both because of their own poor, sloppy choices and because of the poor, careless choices of those who have power over them. This is why I am encouraging people—encouraging you—to write and read daily a Rule of Life that reminds you each day of the good life you want for yourself. We make thousands of choices a day. Many are biological and automatic choices, but many are specific goal-oriented or desire-oriented choices.

For some years, I was a monk in an Episcopal monastery in Cambridge, Massachusetts. I went there wanting conversion. Monks and nuns go to monasteries for their conversion— for becoming more like God. It is a sort of turbo-becoming. Monks or nuns sleep and pray in their cells, spending time there considering their lives. For some, a monastery is the perfect place to live out their calling, to live the life God is calling us to embrace.

But most of us are not monastics. And yet we long for union with God and to become better humans. We also have our inner children, voices wanting more or "other" and needing to be parented. A Rule of Life is, in its own way, an inner-child parenting tool, and it can be an effective one, because we wrote it to and for ourselves. What is the best way to get someone to do something? Make them believe they came up with the idea themselves. That is one of the reasons why a

Rule of Life is so valuable: You wrote it. This is not some set of rules somebody else wrote for you to follow. You wrote a Rule of Life, and it reminds you of your own hopes for your own best self and best-lived life.

Chapter 2

How Monks Do It

We get the Rule of Life "technology" from thousands of years of monks and nuns who lived centered, focused, productive lives because they listened to a Rule of Life that they themselves helped write, or that they deeply respected and chose. Each morning they turned the page. Each morning they were reminded of another chapter full of wisdom that kept them on point. So why should they have all the fun?! Why not import this amazing technology into our lives?

For most of my life, I wanted to be a monk. I experienced a conversion at the age of nine in an empty church, and for many years, I attended church without my parents. As a child, I was a cathedral chorister—a tiny boy soprano with a voice clear as crystal. I would often go to my room and listen to choral music with my body on the bed and my knees up, supporting the record jacket cover of music from an English church called Paisley Abbey. This Scottish abbey was founded in 1163 and was literally the cradle of the Stewart Dynasty. Robert II was born on the premises. His mother, Princess Marjory, fell off her horse when riding to the abbey and was found dead—but by a posthumous operation, the child was delivered and lived to become the first of the Stewart kings. I sat with the abbey's recording on my lap and imagined what it would have been like, before the Reformation, for monks to wander that candlelit nave. And, as a child of alcoholics, in a dysfunctional home, I wondered if there was a place of safety where I could spend time alone and with God. Even as a child, I saw my parents making bad choices for themselves and for me, and I wondered how these bad choices would end.

The bad choices ended the day I began to read the Rule of Life I wrote for myself. That is the day it ended. That one day. An early interest in calligraphy (I'm not kidding!), silence, authenticity, and Jesus all served to clarify a call to test monastic life. Becoming a monk at age thirty-eight and then leaving the monastery after the novitiate is a delicious story for another time. But suffice it to say that while I was visiting and then living in a monastery, I became curious about the Rule of Life, this "life technology" that the monks used to great effect.

The Chapter House

My first exposure to the monastic Rule was as a teenager traveling in Europe. While my friends went barhopping, I found myself going church and cathedral hopping. I was a bit of a nerd! I loved the history behind the European cathedrals, and I was fascinated by the monks who founded (and lived in) them between the tenth and fifteenth centuries. These cathedrals were small cities unto themselves, amazing examples of architecture serving function. For instance, if you visit one of the great English cathedrals today such as Salisbury, Wells, Lincoln, Westminster Abbey, or Canterbury, you will find a room called the "Chapter House." Often an octagonal or round room just off the cathedral's nave, the monks have, over the centuries, used the room for reading a chapter each day of their Rule of Life (hence, the name "Chapter House"). Each order had their own Rule. The Benedictine Rule is the best-known Rule of Life today. The Franciscans had a Rule.

The Augustinians had one. The Cistercians had one. Even those in the Qumran community in Jesus' day had a Rule.

In the Chapter Room, each monk would have his own chair, and usually they would sit in order of rank and seniority. Because of the shape of the room, the monks could see one another, as if sitting around the circle of a campfire. Their actions recalled an ancient practice of people gathering around a fire with their backs to the cold. Since human beings stood up on legs, and Gorg or Thurg or Igor invented fire, people have gathered in circles to tell their stories. And sharing their stories was important, essential even. By telling their stories, they learned how to live and how to stay alive. They shared their experiences of dangers—wild rivers, wilder animals—and opportunities—fresh berries, dry shelter. The campfire story is the ancestor to the self-help book.

Little has changed two millennia later. Monks still gather in a circle, reminding each other of the best choices for life by reading a daily "chapter" of their Rule of Life. Then they go into their day with those words ringing gently in their mind. Remember. Remember. Remember.

Chapters in a Monastery

Terce is an intimate event in the daily life of a monastic community. The monks wake at 5 a.m. It is still quiet, part of "The Great Silence" during which no speaking or work is done. The monks sit silently in their chairs in the darkness of the morning and chant the Morning Office. This short service offers praise for surviving the night, a holdover from a time when surviving the night was a big deal. You were blessed indeed if you weren't facing a plague, fire, Visigoths, Vikings, or starvation.

After morning prayer, the monks spend an hour in silence, share Holy Eucharist, and then partake of a silent breakfast. Only then is the first un-liturgical sound made: during Terce, the monks read from the Rule of Life, which begins the active business of the day. Reading a chapter from the community's Rule of Life starts the day off with a reminder of the community's hope for itself.

On one day, we read a chapter on health. Another day, we read a chapter on money. Some other day, we read a chapter on prayer, and so on and so on and so on. Day after day, we turn the page of the Rule of Life book, chapter after chapter, reminder after reminder.

I lived briefly at The Society of Saint John the Evangelist in Boston, Massachusetts. Their Rule had forty-nine chapters. Or, said in a different way, a book they wrote had forty-nine topics they wanted to remember about how they wanted to live together and live for God. During my time there (and this practice began long before my involvement and continues today), the monks would sit in a boxed circle and read the Rule aloud—one topic each day, then, after reaching chapter forty-nine, begin again with chapter one.

Did we meet the heights of perfection written in our Rule every day? No. Not even close. But the reminders were valuable, and hearing those chapters day after day had an effect on that day's choices. Furthermore, over time, it all sunk into our bones like cherries soaking in vodka. The good reminders of those chapters, read and re-read over and over again, infused us with hope, and we carried our hopes around with us.

From Monastery Rule to My Rule

At The Society of Saint John the Evangelist, we gathered for the reading of the Rule in a very simple, white-washed chapel in the basement. There were aesthetically uncomplicated stall seats, side by side, around three walls. At the open end of the "U" was an icon of Jesus and John, the Beloved Disciple. Jesus completed the circle. The chapel is generally off-limits to the 5,000 guests who come to the monastery to make retreats, and so it was a very intimate space for the brothers to be "family" together. Each chapter reminded us of how we had all agreed to live that particular aspect of life as a monk.

Ultimately, I realized I needed to leave the monastery. When I entered the monastery, I sold all of my possessions and gave away most of my money. I left with just a few trunks to begin a new life. This leave-taking became the impetus for this book.

I packed one of the monastery's Rule of Life books, and every day I read a chapter. In hotels. In my sister's house. In the homes of friends. All the while, I was trying to figure out what to do with my life. I no longer wore a monk's habit. I no longer sat in the monastery, fed and clothed. I had to make my own money. I had to figure out what was next for me. And then, one day, while reading the society's Rule, I wondered: "Why am I reading chapters that applied to the monks? I am no longer a monk there. Sure, the language of the society's Rule was gorgeous, and the chapters of their Rule are challenging and helpful to any reader. But why couldn't I write my own Rule?"

Couldn't I determine the topics for which I needed monthly direction? Why not craft my own Rule of Life to guide me in a new monasticism? And so I did.

That decision has made my life beautiful and courageous—on most days. I invite you to take this same journey. By the time we are done, you will have written your own Rule of Life. And over the years you will edit it and change it for new seasons of your life.

But beware, Kind Reader. A Rule of Life is like Jesus. It will never leave you free to run your life in circles of meaningless choices. It will channel you. It will push you onto a roller coaster. A Rule of Life will send you deeply into the spiritual life, and it will transform and transfigure you. Sometimes you will find it hard to hear your own words in one chapter or another. You may read the words you have written about health or work or friendship or study or exercise or savings or whatever and realize that this hope you have written for yourself is not happening. You will notice you have wandered off track. You will read a chapter about some aspect of your life and think: "Oh my! I am not living this way at all! Where did I step off the path?"

But there's wonderful news even in this discovery. If you have thirty chapters in your Rule of Life, then you are only, at most, twenty-nine days off-track! The old, good, chosen path is there, and because you are reading your Rule of Life, reminding yourself of your life's longings, you only need a small adjustment to get back on your track. Perhaps in reading a chapter in your Rule about health, you realize that you have been binge eating and binge TV watching. As you re-read your Rule and recommit to this hope you have established for your life, you respond afresh, following an old Buddhist saying, "Start from where you are." Get up, brush off the bright orange Cheetos dust, and start eating well and walking daily. The Rule of Life has done its work. You are reminded. You are stepping back on track.

A Word about Failure

There are, admittedly, some chapters of my Rule that stand as a witness and reminder of a better, longed-for life for years…YEARS! Month after month, year after year, I read the chapter(s) and month after month, year after year, I fail to reach some longed-for hope in my life. But those discerned, written chapters in my Rule—even though I fail at parts of them over and over and over again—are essential to my life and to my commitment to live by a Rule of Life.

No life is perfect. We all have weaknesses and failings. The failings are not the problem. The problem is in not being awake and aware that they are areas of failure. Remember the image of the Post-it note: *Note to self: Remember to keep trying...even though you frequently fail at this.*

If we use our Rule of Life as a whipping post, we have misused it terribly. There are already too many of those. The Rule keeps us aware and even optimistic.

And then sometimes, you will see a breakthrough. You will fail and fail and fail because the cosmos keeps handing it back to you until you learn what you need to learn. And then, a wonderful thing will happen. You will read that chapter of your Rule one day, and you will see that issue over which you have been stumbling and failing for years, and suddenly you will read it in a new way. You have finally learned your lesson, and you have finally done that thing well. You have followed your longings for your life. Your Rule of Life has succeeded where hundreds of New Year's resolutions have failed.

Chapter 3

You Can Do It

The Rule of Life, and its various one-page chapters, remind us of how we hope to live. This reminder is not a bony finger pointed at our faces, shooting accusatory lightning bolts of guilt. Rather, these chapters are signs like those on a hiking trail, guiding you on the journey. *This is the path you are on. Was this the path you meant to take?*

The path of a three-hour hike is fine—unless you had intended to be on another path that only takes an hour. If you had planned to be on the green trail because it leads back to where you parked your car, then the red trail, scenic as it might be, will not be helpful. We write and live by a Rule of Life in order to contain and focus our steps in a right direction.

Why Write Your Own Rule?

As we discussed earlier, a number of Rules already exist: Franciscan, Benedictine, The Society of Saint John the Evangelist. So why do I encourage you to take the time and trouble to write your own Rule of Life? Why not just pick an already existing Rule?

You write your own Rule because it will lead you on the path that you've chosen. It will shine light on your hope, and when you stray, your own Rule will be a gentle and clear reminder to step back onto the pathway.

I wish I could tell you I always like reading each chapter every day. I do not. In fact, sometimes I hate it. Sometimes I find myself on a binge, watching *Game of Thrones* episodes one after the next after the next, lying on my bed like Jabba the Hutt with a bowl of jelly beans on my stomach and the remote glued to my hand. Then I read my chapter about health, about my hopes for nutrition and exercise and creativity. What I have written for this subject is in bold contrast to how I have spent my day.

So I make a course correction. I arrive home the next day, and I do not watch TV all night. I bake fish; I walk with my dog. I make a few mugs on the pottery wheel. I go to bed early. The Rule has done its job. I have remembered.

If we own the rules we live by, we will be more likely to follow them. My Rule of Life works well, in part, because I wrote it for my life. I am not slavishly following some arbitrary set of guidelines established by someone else. I took time to consider my life, to acknowledge what worked well within this one life God gave to me. I noticed what could be improved, and then I wrote a Rule of Life that is a perfect fit for me.

Since I wrote this Rule, I am more likely to welcome and heed it when the Rule reminds me that what I am doing—though perhaps fun—is not in my best interest.

This technology of a Rule of Life is not distinctly Christian. One of the earliest uses of a Rule of Life was by the Jewish community in Qumran a couple thousand years ago. A Jew or a Christian or an atheist could use this technology, and one day I hope to write a book on a Rule of Life for those communities too, complete with different language. A Rule of Life allows for the inclusion of one's religious faith and is supported by it, but living by a Rule does not depend on a certain faith. Like any map, it is simply a decided path, be it through a church, a school, or museum. A map is a map on a specific land. A Rule is a rule for a specific life.

Although a Rule of Life can be used by anyone who believes in a higher power, I am writing specifically for a Christian audience. My Rule is deeply guided by my experiences in churches and monasteries. It is rooted in my belief in God and in my love for Jesus. I pray that your Rule will be so as well.

What a Rule Is Not

We have spent some significant time defining a Rule of Life. It is, in short, a map that we check daily to see if we are on the path we have chosen or if we have wandered down an alley or taken an unfortunate shortcut.

It might be helpful to also discuss what a Rule of Life is not. First, a Rule of Life is not a permanent and forever document that once written will never be revisited or revised. I have found that from time to time, I need to edit my Rule. I have to adjust paragraphs and sometimes rewrite whole chapters with respect to changes of life and circumstance. When I hit my mid-forties, for example, my chapter on food had to be rewritten to accommodate a changed physiology. My metabolism had slowed with age, and some refinement needed to be made in my Rule so that I could maintain a healthy weight.

A Rule of Life is limiting, but it is not confining. Let me explain. Limitations we place on ourselves can be cozy and even comforting. Perhaps you have driven over a high bridge and found security in the guardrails. They are not your enemy; the guardrails are not there to deny you freedom. They confine you but in a good way, helping you to move forward, not sideways and perhaps flying into an abyss. Your Rule will help you define your own limits: what you want from your life and what seems to be in line with what appears to be God's hope for your life.

The awareness that a part or parts of your life are off track will be easier to bear and easier to see and correct if you do not find yourself too far down the wrong path when you look up, look around, and ask yourself: "Is this where I really wanted to be? Is this truly the direction that is best for me?"

A Rule of Life will not stop bad things from happening to you. But it will help you to contain the blast. It will be the firm foundation on which you can stand even if you hit bottom. And occasionally you will. I know I have.

A Solution, Not a Resolution

We as a society tend to make New Year's resolutions. We say things like: "This year, I am going to lose those extra pounds!" or "This year, I am going to spend more time resting!" or "This year, I am going to have regular date nights with my spouse!" We sit up and look around like a groundhog checking on the status of the seasons by popping his head out of his hole. On December 29, we consider our life, and on January 1, we make huge pronouncements of corrective behavior. We buy gym memberships or download time-management software or go on a rampage of tossing out candy and chips or cigarettes.

And if you are anything like me, it works. For a while. I become the newly converted enthusiast, nearly a terrorist, not only becoming avid in reforming my own life but also making sweeping pronouncements to those around me as if I am some life-management prophet bent on evangelizing a fat, time-wasting world. With the gym membership and new workout clothes and water bottle and the weight-loss chart pasted on the inside of my medicine cabinet, I am deeply committed. Until February.

Then my new favorite show moves to 10 p.m., so I start going to bed at 11:30. And I am too tired to get up at 5 a.m., so by the time I drive by the gym, it's almost 7 a.m., so I swing into McDonald's for a sausage-and-egg biscuit. While I'm eating, I consider how much needs to be done at work, and before I know it, I pull into the office parking lot fifteen minutes early, my gym bag sitting in the backseat as a throbbing reminder of failed New Year's resolutions.

One of my first adult jobs was in the corporate office of a metropolitan YMCA where I supervised fundraising, communications, and marketing. The budget of a YMCA is based on funds raised and memberships purchased. And each year in January, the media campaign targeted people who had overindulged from Thanksgiving through Christmas.

As we built our corporate budget, we also planned for the inevitability that a certain (rather large) percentage of well-meaning people would do what they had always done in the past—pay dues but not attend. The first few months of the year might be crowded in the workout rooms, but come April and May and the rest of the year, we could anticipate the numbers would wane even though we would still receive significant income from monthly membership fees.

People find it hard to do what they know is good for them. We humans have the tendency to wander from our own vision for our lives, and in some cases, we never even create a vision for our lives. We can't simply look at our hopes once a year. We need to look at them daily.

A Rule of Life is not a New Year's resolution—it's a solution. Here is how it is done.

PART II

WRITING YOUR RULE
OF LIFE

Chapter 4

Getting Started

"If you know God, you know that God's primary activity is giving birth."

—Meister Eckhart
Theologian and philosopher

Everything needs a first draft. And every first draft needs a beginning. Before you can begin the meat of your Rule of Life, you need to determine the structure. Essentially you need to determine the table of contents, the chapters for your Rule of Life. These chapters are the areas in which you desire a daily reminder of how you wish to live. They may include home, worship, study, rest, playfulness, prayer, church involvement, friendship, money, food, mindfulness, conflict, marriage (if you are in one), relational boundaries, etc.

I suggest spending some time on developing an initial list of possible chapters and then letting the list sit for a while, perhaps a few days or weeks. During that time, you may find that some chapter titles seem less important and others materialize with new urgency and awareness. You can have any number of chapters in your Rule of Life. Saint Francis is attributed with the valuable saying "Do few things well," and this applies here. If you have seven chapters in your Rule, then you only have seven issues you are working with and so every seven days, you will begin again at the beginning and will be able to read and reflect on your entire Rule in a week's time. This number of chapters allows you to work hard on seven issues, but after a few weeks, the Rule might start to feel repetitive. I recommend to readers to start with thirty chapters for their Rule of Life.

What would your list of thirty chapters look like? You might start with topics such as health, money, intimacy, prayer, friendship, rest, family, creativity, meditation, yoga, play, sex, loss, and envy. Try making your own list. Once you've selected your topics (chapter titles), you have an outline for your Rule of Life!

In the next part of this book I will walk with you through six broad categories, with a total of thirty chapters. Over time they may not be your best categories or topics and that is fine. What is important is that you eventually develop your own Rule; time and your own experience will tell you which chapters you need to add, delete, or alter. Think of the thirty topics as guides for your guide, from someone who has been down the road before you. In the end, what matters for your Rule of Life is that it contains the chapters you need.

Once you have your list, you can start writing your chapters, realizing that at any time along the way you can delete and add chapter titles as you begin working with the material of your life.

First Steps

The hardest thing about writing is moving past the anxious feeling that you do not know what to write. You do not need to be a great writer, or even a good writer, to write your Rule of Life. You just need to do a few things over and over until it is written.

- Set aside time in solitude and silence for your writing. Thirty minutes is enough and an hour is great. Find a place in your home where you can write and think. A candle often helps set the mood. Find a chair, desk, or comfy seat where you will return daily to write your Rule. Leave your supplies there so that you always return to this spot. Try not to use your traditional office if you work from home.

- Ask God for inspiration and presence.

- Protect yourself from distractions. Turn off anything that beeps, especially your cell phone. If you live with others, sit down with them and talk about the project. While I offer suggestions in the back of the book about ways to develop a Rule of Life for couples, families, and churches, the focus in this part of the text is developing a personal Rule of Life. Ask them not to interrupt you while you are thinking, drafting, writing, and editing. You are making a map for your life. This work is important. You deserve this bold move forward in your spiritual life and your family, friends, and coworkers will thank you for it later. So be clear, set your boundaries, and maintain them. They can live without you for thirty or sixty minutes a day. (And if not, then write your first chapter on boundaries!)

- If you hit a writer's block, quiet your mind, take a deep breath, exhale three times slowly, and then begin to write something. ANYTHING. Just write about the subject in a stream of consciousness. Push through, the way runners run through a cramp. Keep going.

- Do not edit while you write. Just write. Try to write a page. If you write too many words, no problem. Edit later. But write! Do not worry about grammar; spelling can be corrected later.

- Do not push yourself to do too much on any given day (especially if you are prone to overworking). This is a document you will use and edit for the rest of your life. Take your time. A season of three to twelve weeks often gets the job done.

Using Quotations

When I wrote my chapters, I often selected some quotations as a starting point for inspiration. Reading what authors and great thinkers have written about a topic may help you define and craft your Rule. A quick internet search will yield plenty of material. I recommend choosing only one or two quotes to inspire each chapter—but read several so that you begin to think in different ways about the subject.

At the same time, don't go overboard on using quotations of other writers or it's no longer your work. The key to a Rule of Life is to make it a short, readable (and re-readable) letter to yourself. But a shimmering quote or two can perhaps inspire your own note to self. These quotations help me. Sometimes I read an article or two on a subject before writing because I want to learn a few things first!

You will find that you will tend to quote your favorite writers in your Rule. That's okay. I often return to Jesus, of course, as

well as the Buddhist teacher Pema Chödrön; the Celtic mystic
John O' Donohue, the Victorian author Charles Dickens; the
potter M.C. Richards; and the Celtic theologian John Philip
Newell, among others. These writers resonate with me so
they appear in my Rule and my writings a lot. You will find
your own writers to quote.

As an example, I have included some quotes on silence that
inspired me as I was writing my chapter on silence. As you
will see in the next pages, my chapter on silence only uses a
few quotations, but I reviewed several until I found the ones
that most spoke to the heart of my chapter.

*"We need to find God, and he cannot be found in noise and
restlessness. God is the friend of silence. See how nature—
trees, flowers, grass—grows in silence; see the stars, the moon
and the sun, how they move in silence...We need silence to be
able to touch souls."*

—Mother Teresa
20th-century Roman Catholic
nun and missionary

*"Out beyond ideas of wrongdoing and rightdoing there is a
field. I'll meet you there. When the soul lies down in that grass
the world is too full to talk about."*

—Rumi
13th-century Persian poet

*"God is hidden within me. I find him by hiding in the silence
in which he is concealed."*

—Thomas Merton
20th-century Trappist
monk and author

"Anything you want to ask a teacher, ask yourself, and wait for the answer in silence."

—Byron Katie
Contemporary speaker and author

"It is strange to be here. The mystery never leaves you alone. Behind your image, below your words, above your thoughts, the silence of another world waits. A world lives within you. No one else can bring you news of this inner world."

—John O'Donohue
20th-century Celtic theologian

"Silence is Golden; it has divine power and immense energy. Try to pay more attention to the silence than to the sounds. Paying attention to outer silence creates inner silence: the mind becomes still. Every sound is born out of silence, dies back into silence, and during its life span is surrounded by silence. Silence enables the sound to be. It is an intrinsic but un-manifested part of every sound, every musical note, every song, and every word. The un-manifested is present in this world as silence. All you have to do is pay attention to it."

—Eckhart Tolle
Contemporary speaker and author

"The silence is all there is. It is the alpha and the omega. It is God's brooding over the face of the waters; it is the blended note of the ten thousand things, the whine of wings. You take a step in the right direction to pray to this silence, and even to address the prayer to 'World.' Distinctions blur. Quit your tents. Pray without ceasing."

—Annie Dillard
Contemporary speaker and author

"Prayer is then not just a formula of words or a series of desires springing up in the heart—it is the orientation of our whole body, mind, and spirit to God in silence, attention, and adoration."

—Thomas Merton,
20th-century Trappist
monk and author

Study Questions for a Draft Chapter

Here are some common but important questions to ask as you consider the content of each chapter on your Rule. Here, we are considering the topic of silence, but these questions work with any topic.

1. **What do you see in scripture, church tradition, or reason regarding this topic?**

   • What comes up in an internet search on your title? If you are preparing to write a chapter on silence, then simply type the word into a search engine and wander those fields. Pick a bouquet of those offerings, and harvest a few ideas, phrases, quotations, and perspectives.

   • Choose a few people who resonate with you, writers you love and who have informed your life, and research what they have said about silence or whatever chapter/topic you are working on. If you love a famous rock star who has never said anything intelligent about silence well, okay. Move on and see what your favorite preacher has said or your favorite poet or your favorite novelist.

• What do you see in the lives of others—family, friends, colleagues—regarding this topic? For example, if you know someone whose life you deeply respect, go ahead and ask them, "What role does silence play in your life?" They will share their wisdom with you, they will appreciate their opinion being asked, and you will glean valuable data for your writing. Then, every thirty days or so, when you return to this chapter and read phrases that emerged from the conversation, you will think of the person and their good influence on your life.

2. **What do you see in yourself regarding this topic?**

• What do you think about this topic?

• What is your own wisdom formed from your own life? You have some! Trust yourself and dig into your thoughts to find out what you think. Your views on each chapter of your Rule of Life are foundational.

• Where do you succeed? How do you find this topic appearing in your life? What was the best experience you have ever had when experiencing silence (or your current chapter focus)?

• Where do you fail? What keeps coming up as a failure regarding this topic in your own life? I fail at silence every time I turn on the television without a specific entertainment in mind. The same can be said of food or the internet or friendships. Is what we are choosing being carefully chosen or are we living a scatter-shot life? A Rule of Life helps us by fine-tuning, discerning, and narrowing, so that our lives are curated by us, for us.

- What helps you to be your best self in this subject? What benefits come from this way of living? How does having this in my life make it a better life? Why would better living result from having more of this and less of the alternative?

3. **What are your goals for how your life will express this topic?**

   - Writing a Rule of Life is like creating a map. You are writing down a series of statements that you will use to encourage your life in a certain direction. Living with this kind of intentionality is countercultural and takes great courage. If you say yes to one thing, then you are necessarily saying no to something else—many things probably—and this will require courage and tenacity and sometimes, a measure of grief and loss.

   - A Rule of Life is the work of living a self-guided, informed life. It is a matter of determining a set of yes statements and then re-reading them day after day as consistent reminders to stay on the pathway you have determined. Other pathways are not necessarily bad. Your no's might be good for other people, but a Rule of Life says, "This is my path, and I am going to follow it daily." Your no might even have been, at one time in your life, an enthusiastic yes but not these days. Not now, not today.

   - Imagine the tree that you want to become. Then imagine its branches, its soil, its light, its climate, its need for water, and especially its fruit. Don't look at the tree you are now: Look at the tree you want to become. You already have much of what you need to grow and thrive, but some adjustments will need to be made in order to get your tree to be like the one you imagine. Some lovely branches will need to be trimmed for better growth of others. Some waterways may need to be diverted to feed your roots better. Other trees may need to be cut down or replanted elsewhere for your tree to get the sunlight it needs. Adjustment in fertilizer and harvest schedules may be required, and although you may enjoy people climbing the tree for delight, you might have to set down some restrictions against spiked boots.

4. **What measures will you take to encourage the goals you have set for yourself (people, resources, checks and balances, boundaries, etc.)?**

- This can be a sobering question because it implies change, and we humans often are afraid of change. We don't like vulnerability. Even though we agree with Einstein in his observation that insanity is best defined as doing the same thing over and over again and hoping for a different outcome, we humans frequently would rather welcome insanity than embrace change.

- The Christian life is not a spa; it is a gymnasium. Christian formation is a matter of becoming the person you are being called into by God—your best self but not necessarily your easiest self.

- Monks and nuns enter monasteries for many reasons, but one constant is their desire for conversion. Some Christian traditions get squeamish about the word "conversion." But in this context, I define conversion as an event strung over minutes, hours, days, and

years wherein we work to recapture and become
what we truly are. We are uncovering the goodness of
ourselves, similar to the way Jewish mystics explain
the human condition as shards of broken pottery
lamps, each filled with light and yet many covered in
mud from the initial crash.

• What if you find yourself constantly doing things
  that get in the way of your becoming your best self?
  Perhaps you often binge watch TV, wasting eight hours
  at a time and feeling terrible afterward. You want to be
  the kind of person who does not binge watch but can
  still enjoy television and resting from time to time. You
  might set a goal in your chapter on rest and relaxation
  that mentions watching television in moderation and
  within other pursuits like exercising and socializing.
  With your Rule of Life coaching you regularly on this
  topic, it will be nearly impossible to forget who you
  want to become.

• Will it be hard to change? Perhaps. Probably not as hard
  as you think but yes, you are leaving one way behind
  and taking hold of another. You may even spend some
  weeks in a kind of emotional detox in which you long
  for the days when you spent hours watching multiple
  episodes of a TV show. After Moses led the Israelites
  out of Egypt, they wailed and wanted to return to the
  onions they ate when they were slaves. The Promised
  Land is your best self—even if it takes a long time to get
  there. And your Rule of Life is a pathway to wholeness,
  a self-actualizing document of enormous power.

5. What do you seek from God in assistance regarding this topic?

- If you are going to radically change your life by imagining, drafting, writing, editing and reading daily your Rule of Life, then praying for God's guidance is a good plan. A city planner might make a map of the city, but a smart one will have a geologist nearby for close consultation.

- Christians believe God is near and so too is God's Kingdom. We believe that God is busy co-creating life and the world (all our destructive behaviors not withstanding.) So what we do is pray, asking God to be present and to intercede as God chooses. We pray prayers of lament like Psalm 55 when we are in pain. We also make statements to God in our prayers which state what we think, what we long for, and what disappoints us. And in the end we ask God for help. You might include these prayers in your Rule of Life, ones that you find from sources such as *The Book of Common Prayer* or ones that you write yourself.

Final Thoughts

Once you have reviewed these questions on a certain subject, you may be ready to outline and write a chapter. I offer some final words of advice.

Before you begin to write your own chapter, go back to your notes on the subject, the clippings you have assembled from your research, and your thoughts and responses to the list of questions. I keep a paper file on each chapter so that when I see things I like—lines from sermons, conversations, or articles—I can drop them into the file. Later, when I am writing or rewriting a chapter of my Rule, I can go to the file and find waiting for me all of this lovely material.

Use a critical eye. Do not include everything just because it presents itself. Look it over. Wait on the Holy Spirit. Offer it all up to God and to your conscious and subconscious and see what seems to emerge, what stands out and seems to be throbbing to be placed within your Rule. ("Pick me! Pick me!" some passages will seem to shout as you prepare to write your chapter.) Do not linger so long that you never actually get to writing your First Draft (or SFD — "Sh**ty First Draft," a term coined by author Elizabeth Gilbert in her book *Big Magic*). You can always go back and edit later, but get a chapter down on paper even if you need simply to write what you are thinking, and then insert the favored quotes later.

Many people start a Rule of Life and are very energetic (nearly manic) writing their first five or ten chapters, then they burn out and drop the whole thing in exasperation. No need. Relax. It takes weeks to write an owner's manual for a kitchen mixer, and you are far more complex and valuable. Just write two or three or five days a week for twenty to sixty minutes per chapter topic. If you want to go back and edit or expand, so be it, but first, start and finish one full draft of your Rule. Keep at it. Do not stop until you have written out all the chapters you intended. Do not fall to the sin of pride so that you never finish it, and do not fall to the sin of sloth or the grief of fear so that you never really start it. If you think you may blow off your own deadlines, then ask a friend, mentor, or spiritual guide to hold you accountable to the finished product.

Once you write your first draft, you will be so excited about this new tool in your life that you will enjoy the editing and the reading of it. Once you have your thirty chapters, simply write or print them, three-hole punch the papers, and place the pages in a binder. This lets you replace pages with revised rewrites. I also suggest taping a big red ribbon to the top of the binder's spine to use as a daily marker, moving it to the next chapter at the end of the day's reading. When you finish the thirty chapters, lift the ribbon, return it to chapter one, and begin re-reading.

There are other threats to a Rule of Life. One is the need for it to be perfect. You want to craft a great work of art and so you write it into the ground, never completing it and moving on. The second threat is that you try to include everything every human has ever thought on each chapter subject, and so make the chapters so long and cumbersome and stilted that reading it each morning softens your Cheerios.

Do not be seduced by either of these kinds of writer's blocks. Obsessive writers may try to research everything before writing the first word and then the chapter is an unwieldy nineteen pages. Unhelpful. Impressive but unhelpful. Better to simply write down a dozen bullets on the questions and then bang out 300 to 500 words (definitely not more than 700!). You can always edit later. After you have finished, you might see a chapter that needs a new paragraph or notice a terrible sentence, or come across a section that because of a life change, you want to edit. That's okay. That process can and should come later.

Like a map, this is a living document, and maps change as property lines and roads change, buildings are built, and even when natural or manmade disasters alter a terrain. Get comfortable with change, allow for vulnerability, and do not let perfectionism stall and kill this beautiful idea you have of creating and living by a Rule of Life.

Now, let's get started.

Chapter 5

Writing a Sample Chapter

We need to begin somewhere with a sample chapter. We could use any topic—friendship, health, prayer, money—the list of your options is long; but I am going to suggest we begin with a chapter on silence, since silence is a good thing to have in your life and is foundational to the spiritual life. It is in silence that we will do our best thinking, writing, and praying about our Rule of Life, so why not set the stage by starting with the use of silence and its role in your life? (I honestly believe silence is a critical tool for writing and following a Rule of Life. But if silence totally freaks you out, then choose a different topic but follow the same method.)

Writing a Rule of Life is a spiritual practice and needs a discipline about it. You may wish to begin each writing session with a prayer or by lighting a candle. Some people write best with soft music on in the background. I do sometimes. If that is you, then your silence might include soft, wordless music. I do not recommend trying to write with lots of noise, family life, television, or loud music. We need spacious silence in which to write and think and create without distraction.

In this section, I will model how to go about writing a chapter. You will see my notes, quotations, and thoughts. Feel free to borrow some, adapt others, and most importantly, create your own chapter. This is your Rule of Life! Our first step is to explore the study questions.

Silence

1. What do you see in scripture, church tradition, or reason regarding this topic?

- God spoke his eternal word in silence, and He wishes us to receive his words in silence. —Thomas Merton
- Silence is a constant source of restoration. Yet its healing power does not come cheaply. It depends on our willingness to face all that is within us, light and dark, and to heed all the inner voices that make themselves heard in silence. —The Society of Saint John the Evangelist Rule
- The Greater Silence, a time for healing and hospitality to God. —The Society of Saint John the Evangelist Rule
- Inattention to the distractions of music, careless conversation, texts, emails, and constant pinging.
- It is strange to be here. The mystery never leaves you alone. Behind your image, below your words, above your thoughts, the silence of another world waits. A world lives within you. No one else can bring you news of this inner world. —John O'Donohue

2. What do you see in yourself regarding this topic?

- Preaching God implies silence. If preaching is not born of silence, it is a waste of time. Writing and teaching must be fed by silence or they are a waste of time. There are many declarations made only because

we think other people are expecting us to make them. The silence of God should teach us when to speak and when not to speak. But we cannot bear the thought of that silence, lest it cost us the trust and respect of men.
—Thomas Merton

3. What are your goals for how your life will express this topic?

- I want more silence in my life.
- I hope to create a period of silence each day early in the morning.
- I will ask my family to help preserve my period of silence.
- In the past, I have heard God's still, small voice best when I have silence in my life.
- I want to drive without a radio on, and I want to reduce the dings and pings of my cell phone.

4. What measures will you take to encourage the goals you have set for yourself (people, resources, checks and balances, boundaries, etc.)?

- I will ask my spouse to help me create times of silence.
- I will make a fun project out of having one silent meal a week with my family. We will listen to a book together that night with candles rather than watch TV so we have a kind of visual silence.

5. What do you seek from God in assistance regarding this topic?

- I will ask God to help me. I will pray for the strength to find and keep silence for intimacy with God. I will do this in the morning and not at night when fatigue draws me into sleep.

- I will search the scriptures for what the Bible has to say about silence, and then I will search literature that speaks of silence.
- I will go to spiritual leaders and ask them about how they keep silence in their lives.

Sample Chapter

The next step is crafting a sample chapter. Here is a draft from my own Rule of Life. I invite you to consider how you would write your Rule on the issue of silence.

Silence

The silence of early morning is the gift I give to myself. It often requires that I go to bed early, and so I miss time with people, or watching TV, or working late.

Silence is a source of healing for me. God takes the words of my life, those spoken of me and by me, and heals them, washing them like one would a corpse, with scented oils, some grief, and some gratitude. The manipulative, unkind, untrue words about me from others wash down a holy drain. The words said of me and by me that have blessed somehow remain. Like wheat and chaff, silence does this work if the sitting is intentionally with God. So I make the time (rather than trying to find the time), and I sit in silence, letting God wash my words.

Silence offers me the opportunity to look at my life, which can be hard work. Some things I do and say, I do not want to see. I would rather self-anesthetize with busyness. And God will sometimes, through the Holy Spirit, use a pointer to highlight what is lovely and what stinks. In silence I can learn to be my best self—what the church calls conversion of life. Silence is a time set apart from all technology—a sort of word-fasting, a kind of abstinence.

Silence also offers my life integrity, especially in my vocation as a priest. It is not hard to identify a preacher or religious teacher or pastor who lives little in silence. The silence in my mornings and days, in my retreats and sabbath days, lends my words integrity.

"Preaching God implies silence. If preaching is not born of silence, it is a waste of time. Writing and teaching must be fed by silence, or they are a waste of time. There are many declarations made only because we think other people are expecting us to make them. The silence of God should teach us when to speak and when not to speak. But we cannot bear the thought of that silence, lest it cost us the trust and respect of men."

—Thomas Merton

May the Holy Spirit be my companion, a gift of God to help me in silence-crafting, even mischievous and playful and wise as she is. May I love this world and yet never forget that another parallel kingdom is what I long for as I remember my beloved teacher's words:

"It is strange to be here. The mystery never leaves me alone. Behind my image, below my words, above my thoughts, the silence of another world waits. A world lives within me. No one else can bring me news of this inner world."

—John O'Donohue

PART III

A RULE OF LIFE
FOR YOU

Let's get started now by drafting thirty chapter topics. I've grouped them into six broad categories. We will explore each category in more detail, but the actual chapters are not in this book. I have provided some rationale for why I chose these as model chapters, but I encourage you to determine your own chapters and then write them based on your needs.

As a guide, the book includes questions to consider for each chapter. In addition, I have provided some sample prayers for the different chapters as well as notes of support and encouragement.

The thirty topics, broken into six sections, are:

On Listening
- Silence
- Stillness
- Connection
- Prayer & Meditation
- Anxious Thoughts

On Being
- Love
- Creativity
- Friendship
- Forgiveness
- Sabbath
- Work

On Vulnerability
- Suffering
- Fear
- Uncertainty
- Grief & Loss
- Envy

On Body
- Health
- Play
- Home
- Intimacy, Touch, & Sex

On Thought
- Discernment & Discretion
- Detachment
- Technology & Media
- Study & Formation
- Failure

On Existence
- Kindness
- Beauty
- The Planet
- Money & Philanthropy
- Solitude

Chapter 6

On Listening

We humans live inside God. God is not "out there" but rather is everywhere. Imagine a hot air balloon. That is like God. Now imagine a child's birthday balloon wafting up inside the hot air balloon's opening and into its great cavity. That is like us. We exist in God just as a birthday balloon might float around inside a massive hot air balloon. We, each human. We, each planet. We, everything in the cosmos, live inside God.

It is from within God that we strain to listen for God's voice. Sometimes the membrane separating us from God feels thick like the leather of a cow hide. And sometimes, on rare and wonderful occasions, the membrane feels as thin as a birthday balloon or even thinner—as thin as a bubble made with a hoop and a bar of soap.

We float in God, and we often strain to listen for and to hear God. *What am I supposed to do with this life I have been given? What clues is God leaving to point me this way or that? What people in my life is God speaking through—trying to offer me a word of comfort or challenge?*

The truth is that a book about writing a Rule of Life can begin just about anywhere and with any chapter you like. But if we live in God, and if we believe God is communicating to us, then it is essential that we listen as we live and listen as we write our Rule. If we listen to ourselves, to our mentors and family, to the world around us, and most importantly, to God's still, small voice, then we will hear what we need to hear and write what we need to write.

Earlier we worked on a sample "Silence" chapter. Here we begin in earnest on Listening as the first grouping of a basic Rule, because if we are listening well, then the listening will inform the rest of our chapters. If we are listening, then what we write will be informed by that listening.

Do you want a doctor to give you a diagnosis without checking lab results or inquiring after new medicines? Do you want to be treated by a doctor disconnected from medical journals, from the latest procedures, from double-checking with their colleagues? Do you want to be treated by a doctor who isn't listening? No. You want your doctor to be informed when working to heal your body. Similarly you do not want a coach to be uninformed about your sport, your records, or your goals. So too with the writing of your Rule. You must be informed before and as you write, and you must trust and listen to the Holy Spirit. The root of the word inspiration is a combination of inflowing and spirit. So to be inspired is to be filled with the Holy Spirit. And that filling will deeply transform your Rule. Sometimes the Holy Spirit will whisper, and other times it may seem like the Spirit is actually dictating words to you. But you can't hear the Spirit if you're using earplugs—or if you're too busy to listen.

This is why we begin our Rule with Listening. If we can get clear about listening, then we can write, and if we write inspired from the listening, then we will write good material for our self-coaching statements.

As John recounts in the Gospel, Jesus came to us as the "Word," and we pray for the Living Word to show up when we write. But first we must listen for the Word. This discernment, or holy listening, is a learned discipline, and it requires a set of tools. To listen well, we need silence, stillness, connection, prayer and meditation, and a cessation or limiting of our anxious thoughts. That is why our first grouping of chapter titles is designed around how we hear ourselves and how we hear God.

Chapter Suggestions

Chapter: Silence

Listening, whether to yourself, your thoughts, your God, your past, or your longings requires some measure of silence.

In the last section, we used silence as a model for how to write a chapter, but the topic deserves a word here too as you prepare to write your own version. Monks, as we have said, live inside a greater and lesser silence. The Greater Silence occurs in a monastery between the last night service and the first morning service and is a time for what monks and nuns call recollection—an ancient practice in which the physical silence quiets the chatter in our brains so that we can recollect ourselves.

The Lesser Silence occurs during the day for the monastics; this simply means that unnecessary noise is avoided in favor of enough silence to allow the Holy Spirit to sneak in a few words here and there. We might refrain from turning on a loud television or withdraw our hand from a radio knob in favor of a quiet drive to the store. You may not be a monk or nun but I am convinced we each have one inside us.

What do you want in your chapter on silence? Why do you value it? What scares you about it? What do you hope silence will make possible? Will it allow you to listen to God better? Will it help you to recognize your inner longings? Will it protect you from needless noise so that you can be creative or get more rest? Will a chapter on silence provide valuable boundaries within your family so that you get some me time or will silence help you to think things through so that you make better choices?

Your chapter on silence will provide the foundation for the rest of the listening chapters, both because silence contributes to listening and because we live in such a loud culture. And please note that I am not just talking about audible noise. Silence is interrupted by psychic chatter, internal worries, recycling experiences ("I should have said…" and then, "I wish I had said…") as well as anxious thoughts (a chapter we will discuss later in this section).

Chapter: Stillness

Studies have shown that multitasking reduces our effectiveness, our train of thought, and our clarity of choice. Most of us don't even need these studies to know that this is true in our own lives! Just as with silence, stillness is a foundation for listening: It provides space for focused attention. Too often we are driving a car, trying to make a big decision, and talking on our phones, all at the same time. This is a recipe for disaster and a source of anxiety, accidents, mistakes, and eroded relationships. How many times have you tried to tell a close friend some important thing only to realize that they are listening to a neighboring conversation or glancing at a phone? This lack of stillness creates a lack of connection (another important topic we will cover in this section on listening).

Stillness sets the stage for a kind of listening that facilitates good choices, mental awareness, a focus on messages around you, and the kind of life posture that helps us stay human. Stillness is like the deep ballast of a ship sailing low and steady in the water. Perhaps you have been with a still person. My friend Mary is one. She is alert, brilliant, caring, and gentle, and very, very still. She does one thing at a time, and she pauses between things so that the next choice is discerned carefully—the next move, the next decision, the next words.

Stillness is not so much a matter of standing still like a statue as much as it is a way of being on the planet. The reason it inspires and encourages listening—the reason it is in this section—is that stillness is a posture that welcomes deep listening: to self, to others, and to God.

I visited the Joseph-Volokolamsk Russian Monastery for several weeks in 1990. I was with a small group of young adults from various American Protestant churches to discuss youth ministry with young Russians. The monastery was built to hold and house five hundred monks and staff. By the time 1990 rolled around, only three old monks had weathered and survived the storms of communism—and not one living person was left who had experience in youth ministry. I asked the oldest monk how he had survived the decades of Soviet rule over their monastery. His reply: stillness. He explained, "We monks have lived for seventy years like a fawn in the forest. She walks slowly. She remains still for long and many periods of time. She walks and wanders with great intention. But when she hears the snap of even the smallest twig, she freezes. She stands still and fades into the trees until the 'other' has moved on or it is determined to be safe."

Chapter: Connection

Connection is essential to listening because it is a powerful tool for God in our discernment and conversion. Jesus connected. Indeed Jesus is the incarnation of God's desire to connect with human beings. When people need advice, connection to others provides it. When people are frightened or lost or confused, connection helps them tell and retell the stories that guide each of us back on track.

Connection is a human craving without equal. We see the value of connection when people come to our churches. Some come to church seeking beauty. Some come for the teaching or for the service to the poor and marginalized. Others come for the sacraments. But everyone—everyone—comes to church craving, longing for, and often finding connection.

The importance of storytelling for procreation and continuation of the species is so great that the human body actually secretes hormones and chemicals into the blood stream when a story is heard from beginning to end. This biological reaction encourages us to tell stories, connect, and survive.

When I am in trouble in life, I do two things. First, I get quiet. Second, I find friends with whom to connect. I do not necessarily want their advice or their strategies to overcome my difficulty. I simply want connection.

When we connect, we tell stories, and when we tell stories, we listen for truths that help us to live. Your listening section would do well to include a chapter on how you plan to connect with others.

One other note: the reality is that half of you reading this book are introverts and half are extroverts. The introverts need a chapter in their Rule on connection because they need to make the right connection or they isolate. The extroverts need a chapter on connection in their Rule of Life so that they connect in the right way with the right people.

Chapter: Prayer and Meditation

Listening can be accomplished through prayer and meditation. These are not lumped together carelessly. They are different things altogether. Prayer can include meditation, and meditation can include prayer. Prayer is our conversation with God. Meditation is our reflecting upon some aspect of God or God's world. Both allow for a kind of listening that Christianity has long considered central to the relationship God is determined to develop with humanity.

Mother Teresa once told a reporter who asked what she did with God when she prayed: "I listen." Frustrated with the brief answer, the reporter asked, "Well then, what does God do with you when you pray?" She replied, "He listens."

Prayer can be difficult: Sometimes we hear something we do not want to hear. Meditation, similarly, can lead to our realizing something we do not want to acknowledge. This is why we need a chapter about these practices in our Rule.

Listening to life and to one's own heart in meditation is like walking your soul at night with a flashlight, the way a watchman walks a museum late at night.

How is everything? Is anything out of sorts? Why is that light on? Is there an intruder? Has something been stolen or damaged?

Chapter: Anxious Thoughts

Anxious thoughts are a natural part of our biology. They keep us alert and aware of danger. They can be a help to us, just as pain inspires us to jerk our hand away from a hot stove. We need anxious thoughts to protect ourselves from danger. Dealing boldly and directly with anxious thoughts is essential to spiritual, emotional, ecclesial, societal, relational, and biological well-being. But let's be honest: Anxious thoughts can get out of hand. With the advent of 24-hour news coverage, our fear centers are often overstimulated, and anxious thoughts stew in individuals and create a low-grade, covert depression on a global scale.

Our brains are a bit like computers. If too many documents are on the screens or if too many programs are open and working at once, the computer's ability to process slows down. Satan need not tempt us. Satan needs only to keep us fearful and overanxious.

If our computer-brains did not have so many anxiety-programs running at the same time, what creative wonders and deepening friendships might be possible? Released from anxiety, what could our spirits and minds accomplish?

The body is designed for flight-and-fight response. When we see a saber-toothed tiger, blood rushes from our brains to our legs and we ready for a sprint. We are designed for the thinking part of our brains to shut down and hand the baton over to the lizard-brain when we are anxious. That's okay. But the problem is we are anxious a lot. And we don't want to live with the lizard-brain in control.

So what to do with anxious thoughts? Examine them. Not all at once on an annual retreat and purge. Not all at once in a weekly liturgy during a four-second pause at the confession. But all the time, minute after minute and hour after hour. We need to greet anxious thoughts and de-escalate them the same way Dorothy, the Tinman, the Cowardly Lion, the Scarecrow, and Toto pulled back the curtain in Oz's great and fiery hall to expose a little wizard pulling levers and pushing buttons, frantically trying to frighten people into submission.

Because of the prevalence and danger of anxious thoughts, I recommend your Rule include a core chapter on the subject. I believe anxious thoughts are the new Egypt—and we are the slaves in Egypt. The exodus out of Egypt—the release from this slavery—will take us on a difficult journey, across a desert of examining our thoughts.

Byron Katie, a contemporary anxiety guru, recommends this approach: When we think an anxious thought and decide to take it into consideration, we ask: "Is it true?"If the answer is yes, then we take the next step and ask: "Can I be absolutely sure that it is true?" Usually this will shake our resolve to hold tightly to the anxious thought.

The next question is: "How do I react when I think this thought?" Then: "Who would I be without that thought?" The answer may be "peaceful."

Write a chapter about your anxious thoughts and about addressing these questions. Think of your brain as a city: There are some areas into which you should not go late at night without a flashlight and a friend. If you can master your anxious thoughts and reduce their real estate in your brain, then you will open space for building parks, meditation gardens, and art studios instead.

A chapter on anxious thoughts in your Rule of Life can be a way to plant your flag in a peaceable kingdom in your brain and help you to move from fear and anxiety toward peace and joy.

Next Steps

A creative, inquiring person will think of many possible chapters on the topic of Listening. Other related topics may include discernment, friendship with God, retreats, decluttering, fasting, uncertainty, sleep and dreaming, peaceful homemaking, mornings and evenings, and media consumption. The list could go on and on. But I am suggesting that, for now, you simply begin your Rule of Life with four to six primary chapters under the grouping of Listening. You may decide to choose the ones I suggested (silence, stillness, connection, prayer and meditation, and anxious thoughts) or you may determine that your Rule of Life needs a different mix under the Listening section. That is your decision.

I strongly encourage you to begin with Listening as your first section. Think of the process of moving from one house to another. The best plan, really, is to place rugs first on the floors of the new house. If you unload all the furniture before the rugs are down, you'll have a lot more work to do. This is why

I encourage Listening as the first grouping: In this way you are laying the groundwork (the rugs, so to speak) in order to hear the other chapters emerge.

So pour a cup of good tea or coffee, wine, water, or sparkling cider, turn off your devices, find a comfortable chair, and ask yourself: *If I were to coach myself on listening—listening to myself, listening to God, listening to my life—what five chapters should this first section contain for me to read and re-read five times a month?*

Pick one of the chapter topics and begin an outline using the five study questions from Chapter 5. These can and should be used in the process of discernment as you write each chapter. Here are the questions again:

1. What do you see in scripture, church tradition, or reason regarding this topic?

2. What do you see in yourself regarding these topics?

3. What are your goals for how your life will express this topic?

4. What measures will you take to encourage the goals you have set for yourself (people, resources, checks and balances, boundaries, etc.)?

5. What do you seek from God in assistance regarding these topics?

Study Questions for Draft Chapters

Here are some deeper questions by subject that you might ask as you consider the content of your Listening section.

Silence

See the draft questions and answers in Chapter 5, pages 44-46.

Stillness

- What unnerves or frightens you about stillness?
- What do you need from God in order to be peaceful with stillness?
- What in your life mitigates against stillness and how might you create space, place, and logistics so that you can practice the ancient art of stillness?
- What interrupts your stillness? How might you greet interruptions by overcoming their effects?
- What would it take for you to exercise stillness as a spiritual practice? How can your friends, family, mentors, and God help you?
- Who do you know who seems to have mastered stillness? What have they said or written, or what has been said of them, that might help you follow their lead?

Connection

- What gets in the way of connection for you? What barriers exist to connection in your life, both with God and with humans?
- Under what circumstances does connection work, and how might you get more of that in your life?

- What story do you need to let go of to connect with others or with a group? Who would you be without that story?
- Which people among your friends and mentors or in church history connect well? Seek their advice as you craft statements to include in this chapter.

Prayer and Meditation

- What do you need to begin or maintain a prayer and meditation practice?
- Who do you know from church history or from your present circle of friends who prays or meditates well? What might they teach you that you could include in your Rule as encouragement?
- When have you had success in prayer or meditation? What made this form of listening possible and enjoyable, effective or evocative?
- What logistical barriers exist to prayer or meditation in your life?
- Who would you be without the fear that you "can't" pray or "can't" meditate?

Anxious Thoughts

- What kinds of anxious thoughts do you host in your mind?
- What triggers anxious thoughts for you? These triggers might include a boss, a church group, authority, manipulation, abuse, or an event in your past that you see replayed in your life or another's.
- What do you do when you encounter an anxious thought? Do you have a practice with which you greet it and calm your mind and soul?

- Using Byron Katie's questions, have you been able to mitigate the anxiety?
- Do you need a spiritual or psychological mentor or teacher to help you manage anxious, negative, or fearful thoughts? If so, what needs to be in your chapter that encourages you to seek help?
- Have you had a life experience that created a deep-seated fear? Can you bring that fear to God for healing? How can your chapter help you to remember to do that?
- Do psalms like Psalm 55 help you to feel less alone in your anxious thoughts? How might you craft a chapter on anxious thoughts that will bring comfort to you?

Closing Prayers

Many people end their chapters with a prayer they have written. One type of prayer is called a *collect* because of the way the words collect the various elements of a person's chapter into one prayer. Others prefer to close with a favorite quotation, poem, or even "the top three things to remember." You will want to decide how to close your prayer time for yourself.

Here are some sample prayers for the suggested chapters. Feel free to use them (or parts of the prayers) in your own chapters. *The Book of Common Prayer* offers an array of collects that might be helpful for you. If you would like to write a traditional collect, you might search the internet for the traditional structure or some samples.

A Prayer for Silence

It was in silence, Lord Christ, that you sat with God to listen and in which God listened to you. In silence, you walked to Jerusalem, hung on the cross, and even rose to new life in a dark cave, alone but for an angel or two. We live in a noisy world and a noisy culture. When you said "be in the world but not of the world," you meant the noise of the world. Cover my ears. Kiss my forehead. Remind me that all shall be well and grant me that peace which passes all words. Amen.

A Prayer for Stillness

My primordial nature is to grab and struggle. Just as babies grab the air in an automatic response of fear when awakened, so even now I move in anxious self-protection and nervous inattention. Still my heart and my body, O Christ, so that I might hear your still, small voice telling me that I am beloved of you, for that hearing will still me further, and this cycle will grant me peace. Amen.

A Prayer for Connection

God of all creation, you chose to connect to our planet and to all beings on and within it by becoming flesh and stepping on the earth. You came to be with us, Emmanuel. You connected to us, and it cost you deeply. Take my hand and place it in the hands of those with whom connection will heal me. When I recoil, draw me out. When I wince in shame or turmoil, betrayal or fear, look deep into my eyes and whisper to me. Coax me out like a mouse from a hole so that I may not be alone just as you, O Trinity of Being, are not and have never been alone. I am made in the image of three as one. Help me to live out that image. Amen.

A Prayer for Prayer and Meditation

You taught us to pray and you modeled prayer in the scriptures we read. You taught us to ask the Father or Mother or Spirit for what we want and what we need. Grant me, Jesus, the will and the space in which to find time for prayer in such a busy and noisy world. Renovate my image of you if that image in any way forms a barrier to my connection to you. I want to hear you. I want you to hear me. I want us to listen to each other. Bring me into the house and gate of your presence. Amen.

A Prayer for Anxious Thoughts

There is great comfort in the image of you in the Garden of Gethsemane, for you give me permission to feel fear and to ask if there is any other way. Inspire in me questions that lead me out of my terrors and fears, my regrets and betrayals, my starvations and my prisons, those imposed and self-made. Create in me a well of peace from which to draw and make my Rule of Life a part of that well. Stand with me, Holy Wisdom, in solidarity with Christ and take my hand when it trembles. Hold it. Warm it. Pull me toward your abiding love so that I have the strength to face fears and losses, worries and regrets with that shimmering question: "Is it true?" You are the Word made flesh. Be also the question made flesh, Lord Christ. Amen.

Chapter 7

On Being

Our culture seems to value doing more than being. Given this context, a series of chapters in our Rule on Being seems essential. We need reminders—these notes to self we have written—that we must live well as humans. This series of reminders about our humanity will not come from the advertisers that want us to buy their products or from peers who want us to work. Our reminders on Being must be daily.

We are called human beings but increasingly we are measured by others and ourselves by what we do on the planet instead of who we are. Hundreds of books and apps offer motivation for the to-do list generation so we can complete eleven things before breakfast and another dozen tasks before lunch. If you are like many people, you get a lot accomplished in a day, and in the evening, you zone out in front of the television or with YouTube cat videos, in a dull stupor from pure exhaustion. In earlier times, we did less in the course of the workday and had more energy in the evenings for friendship and personal reflection. But times and expectations have changed. And if you are like me, a work addict, then you do so much that it nearly kills you, harming relationships with others and your own relationship with your body and with God.

Work addiction is not seen as a problem in America because everyone is overworking and the effects are hard to recognize. After all, who doesn't want to accomplish more each day, to complete the checklists, to attract the attention of our superiors for our devoted work ethic? While we have more and more technological resources to ease our work lives, we find that they ironically create an expectation of an around-the-clock worklife. Other addictions raise red flags for our family and friends, but work addictions are respected and even praised. Our addiction to work makes us part of the American machinery.

The effects of doing rather than being are far-reaching. Friendships wither on the vine of overscheduling. Romances and partnerships, marriages and parent-child relationships weaken and crumble with the overstimulation of work, social media, internet surfing, online shopping, and gaming. Careers soar to great heights, even among bishops and clergy, and yet, just beyond the fancy trappings and vestments is a deep exhaustion and frantic pedaling to keep up with expectations—our own and those of others. I speak from my own experience: I have been in this very position.

This work and stimulation addiction separates us from our souls. If evil wanted to harm us, would it not be the best strategy to do so cloaked? Invisibly? Unseen? I would respond instinctively to a person with a gun or a knife. This invisible danger of work addiction attacks in much more subtle ways.

A few years ago I was hit by a street tram in Prague. As a result of the accident, I have lost all sense of smell and taste. If people wanted to harm me, kill me even, all they would have to do is turn on the gas of my stove as I head to bed for a night's sleep. If they wanted some drama, they could light a candle in another room as I slept. I would die by asphyxiation or by explosion, never really knowing I was in danger since I cannot smell the gas.

This is why chapters on Being are so important. Modern evil tempts us to stay busy, overstimulated, overscheduled, and overcaffeinated. We become lost, friendless, divorced, encumbered with too many possessions and commitments and too few healthy relationships.

C.S. Lewis's senior devil Screwtape defines this slow, steady undermining in *The Screwtape Letters:* "Indeed the safest road to Hell is the gradual one—the gentle slope, soft underfoot, without sudden turnings, without milestones, without signposts...Your affectionate uncle, Screwtape."

This is one of the reasons I wrote this book: When we are not paying attention to our "being" but only our "doing," we lose our way in the dark forests of overfunctioning and overworking. And slowly, ever so slowly, our lives are too noisy, and we lose the ability to hear ourselves and to hear God.

I wonder how many people are born, live full, long lives, and then die, never really taking the time to ask themselves key questions about what kind of being they are as humans. By writing chapters in your Rule on Being, you are deliberately thinking about these subjects and asking difficult questions: *How do I want to live? What kind of person do I want to be? What ways of life contribute to being the kind of person I want to be?*

Again, from Screwtape: "It is funny how mortals always picture us as putting things into their minds: in reality our best work is done by keeping things out."

Many of us have a better grasp on how our cell phones work than how our selves work. A Rule of Life can help correct this situation. This section on Being is essential to your soul-work. I suggest that you go slowly and craft part of your Rule on Being after a long and intentional act of mindfulness, of listening.

This process of discernment and mindfulness is why I recommend Listening as the first section in writing a Rule of Life, followed closely by Being. If we are listening and intentionally focused, we can begin to face our vulnerabilities, manage our bodies, consider our thoughts, and wonder about our existence. This process is like triage in a hospital: Medics need to stabilize a body just arrived from a car accident. Once the vital signs are stable, then the medical professionals can move on to stitches, bandages, and surgery. If we create a Rule of Life with carefully discerned chapters on Listening and Being, then the rest of the chapters will flow from that core wellness of listening and being. First, we hear God, and then we hear ourselves. We choose a way forward that infuses life with good Being choices. The rest proceeds and flows out of these two chapters.

This section on Being asks profound questions: *How do I love? How do I create? How do I make, keep, depart from, and manage friendships? How do I forgive and ask for forgiveness? How do I keep the sabbath holy so that I may rest and rejuvenate into being well and whole? How do I work so that I earn what I need but in such a way that I work in order to live rather than live in order to work?*

When we listen to God and our hearts, our Being is transformed: Love manifests, creativity peeks out from the folds of work's skirts, friendship unfolds like a red carpet, and forgiveness is offered and received. Sabbath restores body and soul so that we may love, create, befriend, and forgive with whole hearts.

This section on Being coaches us on the discernment and writing of chapters that are basic to Being. You may have other chapters in your Rule on Being as well.

Chapter Suggestions

Love

This can be a difficult chapter to write. Love is a big, multi-faceted topic. But as people of faith, we follow a God who set love as the basic ingredient of the first two commandments of the Torah—to love God and love neighbor and self. We need to establish a priority on love if we are to live well as human beings. It can be easy to issue a heavy sigh and eyeroll when we see love as a chapter title. It can seem either too syrupy or too big and intimidating. And yet, I encourage you to sit for a few minutes and reflect on love. I suspect that you will find words start flowing quickly.

One suggestion to manage the flow of thoughts is to create an outline of paragraphs. Name your longings for different kinds of love such as the love between friends, partners, close friends, God, and family. You may also make reference to the love you experience and not just the love you offer, defining what love feels good and nourishing and what counterfeit forms of love you may want to flag as unhelpful or hurtful.

Creativity

Made in the image of God as we are, we share many of God's features. God, who is many things and none and all, is chiefly Lover, Creator, and Giver. We are made in that same image, and so we too are lovers, creators, and givers. Human beings are different from other earthly life forms, in part because we make things. Animals make things too—but not like humans. When I was young, my mother would often say she was not creative. She loved things—textiles, pottery, painting, books— but she wished she could create things. I was always astounded that she never considered as creation the six-course Chinese dinners complete with Peking duck, Lion's Head soup, handmade pork and leek dumplings, and Moo Shu pork with homemade pancakes. For her, that was just dinner.

All of us have creativity inside us, and a chapter on creativity is to a Rule of Life as oil is to a car engine—essential and lubricating. If you truly feel that you do not create things, then perhaps your chapter on creativity sets up space to consider creative pursuits. Baking bread, raising a child, writing letters, making a home, hosting a dinner party, having an intimate relationship with your partner, or even doodling during a pathologically dull meeting can all be forms of creativity. The divine spark of creativity inside each of us, if not lit, will smolder and fill us with smoke. So write about your longings, remind yourself that you can and have created, and use your Rule of Life to inspire creativity in your work and home lives.

Friendship

I speak to many people for whom friendship is a challenge. The demands of work and family leave little time for cultivating friendships. Yet friendships can be a source of renewal and companionship. Friendship touches upon many other chapters in this Rule of Life, including love, connection, forgiveness, play, intimacy, and touch.

Describe what needs to happen in your life to facilitate friendships and identify barriers that tend to imperil these relationships. If, for example, overwork gets in the way of friendships, your chapter on friendship will remind you of the need to set aside time for others. With your Rule of Life as a guide, you will never be more than thirty days away from a note to self reminding you of the important work of Being and of friendship.

Forgiveness

I suggest a chapter on forgiveness because it is so necessary for humans. I know from my own experience that the oft-quoted saying, "Withholding forgiveness is like taking poison and hoping another dies from it," is as true as it is annoying. My spiritual director used to say that I "warm myself by the fires of my own resentments." As I age and work hard on my conversion, this is less and less the case, and yet I am aware that I still struggle with forgiveness.

In your chapter on forgiveness, articulate your hopes for forgiveness in your life. *What does withholding forgiveness do to you? What does it feel like when others withhold forgiveness from you? What do you need to do to help un-constipate your soul when forgiveness lodges in your gut and will not break open with a release of love and compassion?*

Another consideration as you write this chapter on forgiveness is to think of a time when you forgave and the results improved your life. Tell yourself that story, remember the success, and offer the hope for more such successes. Forgiveness requires deep self-awareness, profound humility, and the willingness to take your foot off someone's neck. Hatred, revenge, and the like are tempting, but the chapter in your Rule will dismantle those bombs every thirty days—if you let it.

Sabbath

God made all things in heaven and on earth, says Genesis. Each act of creation was named good or very good. However, only one thing was called holy (or hallowed, depending on your Bible translation). The first time this bombshell-of-a-word is used in our scriptures is for the naming of sabbath rest. If God is to attribute rest with such weighty glory, then who am I to do anything other than relent and enjoy it? A chapter on sabbath in a Rule of Life is essential in our society of overwork.

Sabbath is something we "make" and something we "keep," not something we do. Sabbath may be a few minutes of rest with eyes closed at one's desk with the door shut, a day off at home without any chores or needful appointments, a week off on vacation or a season off on sabbatical. Sabbath rest is a commandment—but it is also countercultural to our noisy lives of doing, doing, doing.

The gates of the Dachau concentration camp featured the phrase, "Arbeit macht frei." *Work will set you free.* That was a lie then and it is a lie now. When scripture and early church writers call us to be "in the world and not of the world," they are not referring to the world God created, which is of course, "very good." Rather, they are calling us to avoid a world marked by conspicuous consumption, self-anesthetizing

workaholism, the wasted noise of busyness, and the frantic
lust for power and control. Sabbath rest allows us to slow
down, notice our selves, and see a bigger picture of wellness
of Being.

In my Rule, I try to imagine God content with my work—and
thrilled with my rest. To take time to rest weekly and daily
is an act of humility. It accepts the reality that I am not God.
There is also the challenge of a sabbath day that is genuinely
recreative rather than heavily slothful. To hallow our sabbath is
to fill it with sleep, friends, hobbies, music, and entertainment.
In keeping with the Christian notion that a feast begins at
sunset on the night before, I do not agree to any work on my
sabbath eve unless for pastoral need. At sunset the night before
my sabbath day, I wash my bed sheets and dry them. I then
dress my bed gently, the way a deacon dresses the altar with
the vessels of Holy Eucharist—lovingly, carefully, slowly, and
reverently as a symbol to myself of the need we have for sleep
and rest.

As you write your chapter of your Rule on sabbath-keeping,
consider your hopes for your life. Consider sabbaths of
differing kinds such as minutes (breaks), hours (naps), days
(a day off but not filled by chores), and vacations. Discern
your goals for living sabbath as a well being on the planet
and imagine how that sabbath rest might bless you and
those around you. Then write this longing in a chapter of
your Rule.

Work

We humans work to create things. If we are careless, we
create useless things or even dangerous things. But if we are
mindful, there is little more satisfying than working to make

something of which we are proud and with which we are pleased: a delicious meal for friends, a new program at work, a series of useful tools in a factory, an email or letter that inspires good action.

I take great joy in stepping back from my pottery wheel to look at mugs or bowls I've made for my kitchen. When I throw pots, I am working, yes, but I am also creating. Our work is a form of creativity. Work carefully done is part of being a good lover, creator, and giver. It is part of our *Imago Dei*, how we bear the image of God into the world

But we need to ask ourselves hard questions when we are writing this chapter. I want to work hard but not so hard that I self-anesthetize, avoiding a painful situation and decision. Feeling our pain, looking directly at it, is essential in life. I sometimes use work and busyness to avoid pain. Perhaps you do too.

My chapter on work includes a focus on mindfulness. Is my work producing something about which I am passionate or which is, at least, a good thing in the world? Is it, as the artist Henri Matisse would say, "illuminating the fog" of life or simply making more of it? Is my work in line with the art I want to make in life or is it just a means to money or power or prestige, the three desert temptations of Jesus? I must take great care when saying yes to new work, be it paid or volunteer, so that I can stay true to the other chapters in my Rule, including sabbath, friendship, and love. If I discern that I must say no to new work, I must be willing to feel the pain and loss that may come from that decision. I may need to say no to work that could have been fun or lucrative or impressive, acknowledging that it is not the right fit in my life at the moment but may be perfect for some other person or in some other season of my own life.

In the end, I am curating this one life, given to me daily as
a gift. Work takes a large portion of my wakeful days and so
needs to be carefully discerned. Work also needs boundaries
so that work stays in its stream and does not flood the entire
neighborhood of my life, sending me to the roof, strained in
exhaustion.

When writing your chapter on work, there is no need to go
into detail about your employment as much as the idea of
work. The questions that are more important deal with how
much work you would like to do, how to set (and reset)
boundaries, and naming the trouble that arises with overwork
or neglect of work.

Next Steps

If we can love robustly the right things and people, then we
may be able to love the Lord with all our heart, mind, and soul.
And if we can love well, then there is a chance we may create
a beautiful life. Having created a beautiful life, we have every
possibility of being people who attract, make, and keep friends
who fill our lives with meaning and are icons to the friendship
Jesus makes within and around us.

Regular forgiveness should be a healthy part of our
relationships with partners, friends, and colleagues. And
having forgiven ourselves and one another, we find sabbath
rest and are renewed and refreshed for creative endeavors.

Writing these chapters on Being is very tender work. They
will take thought and discernment. This process will require
us to let go of nostalgia and fantasy and focus on truth with
relentless determination. This is how we make our lives: We
focus on Being.

Spend the time you need to get this section right. Resist the temptation to be intimidated by it. Take one thought, one word, one phrase at a time. The Holy Spirit sits ready with sharpened pencils and plenty of erasers to help you in its creation. You are writing the manifesto of your life and nobody but you can do it. And indeed you can do this. You are doing it right now.

Finally, this section on Being is a huge topic. You may be tempted to write ten or more chapters on Being. Don't. Start with six chapters on Being (even if the chapters aren't the same as those suggested here). As you craft the rest of your Rule, you may come back and discover a glaring omission. But don't let yourself be waylaid here. There is much to come!

These sections on Listening and Being are the bedrock of all the other chapters in a Rule of Life. Jesus came to us not as an idea or figment but as the Word made flesh. So write the words that will inspire you each day to be your best self.

Study Questions for Draft Chapters

Love

- What do you long for when it comes to love in your life?
- What ways of life do you believe inspire and contribute to living a loving life?
- What gets in the way of loving?
- What gets in the way of being loved by others?
- What different kinds of love do you want in your life? What do you need to do to receive that love?
- In what ways do you want to receive God's love? How can your actions inspire that?

Creativity

- What ways do you see creativity emerging from your life? How do you maintain that creativity?
- What tends to interrupt or block your creativity? How might you mitigate these barriers?
- What might your Rule of Life set as goals that could contribute to more creativity in your life?
- Do you remember a time of great creativity? What was going on during this period? What needs to return to your life to reinvigorate this kind of creativity?
- What do you do that might seem basic and dull but, when considered in the right light, is actually a great creative act? (e.g. raising children, working for your paycheck, cooking meals, romance, friendship, some form of art, or even doodling).

Friendship

- What are your longings for friendship in your life?
- What does Jesus' assurance of friendship in John's Gospel mean to you? How does this assurance inspire your desire for friendship with God?
- What gets in the way of or blocks friendship for you? (e.g. overwork, children and family, social discomfort, age, disability, grief or loss, memories of a soured friendship, or the pain of a recent estrangement or dissolution of a friendship).
- What do you want out of friendship? What do you believe you have to offer in friendship?
- What do others say about friendship? (e.g. authors, researchers, spiritual leaders, your current friends).
- How would friendship improve your life?

Forgiveness

- Holding a grudge is like taking poison and hoping another dies from it. Do you have a tendency to anger easily or hold grudges? What do you need from God or other humans in order to be released from these tendencies?
- From whom do you need to seek forgiveness?
- What barriers or thoughts exist in your life that block your forgiveness of another?
- For what do you need to forgive yourself?
- How would forgiveness improve your life?
- What do others say about forgiveness that seem to be great summations of the issue? What quotations might you include in your Rule chapter?

Sabbath

- What is your vision of the perfect sabbath?
- How can you imagine sabbath as a brief rest during the day, in which you feel free to stop and rest?
- What rituals might you observe that could be effective to usher in sabbath time? (My example was making my bed with clean sheets.)
- Identify times when an attempt at sabbath turned into a day that seemed wasted and felt like it hosted a laziness without creativity.
- In what ways do you hope to make your sabbath holy? How can you set aside time without chores so that the sabbath is a delight?
- Is your current observance of sabbath time restful and creative, or is it simply recovery time from the terrors of the previous week and preparatory for the next?
- What do authors and scriptures say about sabbath that inspires you?

Work

- What thoughts and memories may help you recall and reclaim work as a creative and life-giving act?
- What inspiring things do authors and spiritual leaders say about work that you might like to include in your chapter as a source of inspiration?
- What boundaries do you want your chapter to cite so that your work remains something you do to live, rather than your entire life's existence?
- What gentle warnings do you need in order to find a right relationship with work?
- Is there something about your work that fills you with joy? What is there to celebrate? These joys might include income, a product, a ministry, friendships among colleagues, or creative expression.
- What might your chapter say about overwork or work-addiction? What will you say to maintain your awareness regarding overwork?

Closing Prayers

A Prayer for Love
The cosmos lives in love the way fish live in water. We exist in love. We breathe love, and our primary calling is to love God, neighbor, and ourselves. And yet sometimes we hate. Sometimes we withhold love when we are hurt or grief-stricken.

O God, grant us the strength to live such a prayerful existence that we regularly step into the streams and rivers of love that flow from you. You are the lover of our souls, and without your love we would be lifeless stones and clanging cymbals. Seduce us when we are chilled by life's hardships. Enflame our love for each other and this planet and so guide our hearts that we are driven into your love as a moth to its flame. And there, consume us in the love you have for humanity. Amen.

A Prayer for Creativity
From the womb of the Trinity, you created all that is. Inspire us to pour out our creativity as we recall that we have been made, created in your image. When we feel that we lack creativity, alight our natural creativity and infuse us with the muses of your angels. When life hurts and our creativity withers, breathe new waters into dry bones and restore us to our rightful place as beings that create. When we fall short of your heavenly glory, guide our hands back to the center as you would the hands of a potter. Uphold us that we might create beauty, peacefulness, and all that heals a broken world. Amen.

A Prayer for Friendship
You, O Lord God of the Universe, are the One Who Is. You live in friendship and have never not known friendship. You came to be among us, calling us not servants but friends. You sent Jesus Christ to embody friendship and to model its vulnerability. Help us to show up as friends, both to you and to one another. When we betray our friends as your disciples betrayed you at the cross by their absence, help us to forgive ourselves as you have forgiven us. When we feel the searing pain of betrayal in friendship, raise us up and breathe new life into us. And when we are in the midst of great friendship, show us great bounty, so that we waste not a moment of such nectar. Amen.

A Prayer for Forgiveness
Grant us, Lord Christ, the ability to forgive those who harm and betray us. Flush out the sludgy poisons of resentment and fill us with life-giving waters from our baptism, fresh and clean. Breathe into us new air that pushes the smoke of anger from our souls. You have forgiven us. Help us to forgive others.

Help us to forgive ourselves. Cut the chains that bind us in our unforgiveness and take our yoke so that we may rise and run the race to which we are called—a race of new life, unfettered and free. Amen.

A Prayer for Sabbath
The story of our faith begins as Hebrews are released from slavery in Egypt and led to a promised land. We too need this release from the slavery of work and earning. We are tired, overstimulated, overcaffeinated, and overscheduled. We often rest only as recovery and readiness for more work. Grant us such a deep sense of peace that we might consider enough work to be enough. Help us to turn off the dazzling lights of computers and cell phones so that your transfigured light may call us to a new reality. Help us to turn down our beds with liturgical solemnity, and as we sleep, brush us with the kiss of healing so that we may enter a new day with the assurance that all of nature has asked permission to exist and so it has been granted. Amen.

A Prayer for Work
O God of creation, you worked and you rested in the creation of this beautiful planet. Your hand is evident in the moments of our lives as you work through the Holy Spirit to make all things new. Grant us the joyful creativity that infuses our work with your light. Guide our discernment so that our yes is yes and our no is no. Grant us solace when work is to be replaced with rest, and grant us consolation when work is welcomed for the provision of income, the manifestation of creativity and when possible, the benefit of humankind. Grant us the energy to arrive at our work with enthusiasm, and equally the ability to know when our work must be set aside. And assure us that our work, begun and ended in you, will co-create within your creation of life and love. Amen.

Chapter 8

On Vulnerability

"Sorrow prepares you for joy. It violently sweeps everything out of your house, so that new joy can find space to enter. It shakes the yellow leaves from the bough of your heart, so that fresh, green leaves can grow in their place. It pulls up the rotten roots, so that new roots hidden beneath have room to grow. Whatever sorrow shakes from your heart, far better things will take their place."
—Rumi, Islamic scholar and mystic

Your Rule is here to remind you that you are strong, resilient, courageous, and authentic. Yet vulnerabilities will come: betrayal, deep loss, poor life choice, divorce, bankruptcy, cancers, addictions, stubbed toes, insults, and relationships neglected. The list goes on. Avoiding chapters in a Rule of Life about our vulnerability brushes pain under the rug, where it will flop around and ultimately knock you off center. The process of facing your vulnerabilities, your challenges, and painful places will change your life.

The work of thinking about these difficult subjects can be, and often is, as valuable as living by the chapters once they are written. Vulnerability is pride's sentry and humility's midwife.

Vulnerability is a medicine to detoxify pride and break open the hard shells of our ego. Vulnerability—the willingness to be wounded and to feel pain—will take courage, yes. But you also will find a new determination to live life and not hide from it.

Another critical element of vulnerability is its ability to bind us one to another. I connect best with others not by the many and great things I know but rather by my willingness to emphathize: "That hurts, right? I don't know what you are going through, but I have hurt in a similar way, and we can sit together for a while if you want." And people usually do want to sit. Very much. For a long time. In silence for awhile, and then sometimes in story.

When we can meet and tell our stories of vulnerability, to ourselves and to others, we heal. What we know of the ancient human is that we were designed to get through the forests to a campfire. There, around that fire, with the dark forest at our backs, we look into the light, and we tell our stories.

Discussing vulnerability as we prepare to write is essential. As we humans tell or listen to our stories from beginning to end, our bodies have evolved a reward system. Our bodies release oxytocin into our bloodstream. It is both a reward (it feels good, calming, and soothing) and a connector (this is the same chemical secreted into the body of a woman who has just given birth). And so we have a biological response to hearing and telling a story. Why? Because by telling a story about what can happen—in the dark forest and in our lives—we learn how to navigate those places for survival. The oxytocin pumping into our blood when we tell or hear a story is a survival reward, simultaneously soothing us and connecting us to each other.

The discernment and writing of a Rule of Life is countercultural and never more so than when dealing with the subjects in our lives that make us vulnerable. Our society encourages us to avoid confrontation (even within ourselves) and to reach for something to anesthetize pain and discomfort.

Am I feeling the pain of a deep disappointment? Perhaps if I check my emails or texts I will distract myself from feeling the disappointment or anger that was knocking on the door of my reptile brain and about to cause some fear or rage or grief.

We do better in life to face our fears, our hurts, our vulnerabilities, and our losses. A Rule of Life helps us to face these so that even in darkness, we know their contours. In facing our fears and vulnerabilities, we listen to what they can teach us.

Addiction researchers such as Pia Mellody suggest that each person has a community of four inside ourselves—three children curated by an inner adult. Our Rule helps us to manage the inner rantings of those three kids archived deep within us.

The youngest inside us is the wounded child. It screams, rants, and demands because it remembers having no power. These wounds still exist in our adult selves. The next child, the adapted child, is age 7 or 8. This child screams "It's not fair!" a lot, wants to explore, and is a little frightened. The third child is our inner adolescent who acts out by greedily grabbing for more, more, more and by directing anger and rage toward anyone who appears to threaten this way of life. This child wants to stay out late, eat all the pizza, and key the car of the guy who did that mean thing.

And then we have our inner adult. He or she convenes the other three, hosting the conversation. Our inner adult is always saying to the inner baby: "I will get you what you need, and I will protect you." To the inner adapted child: "I know. I am sorry it's not fair. I will not control you, but I am here if you need me. I love you. I will keep you safe." And to our inner adolescent: "I understand that you want these things, that you are angry and want to act out in anger, but I love you too much to let you do these things."

When we are vulnerable, our inner children tend to have a lot to say. Our inner baby wails, our inner adaptive child freaks out, and our inner adolescent grabs the keys, the credit cards, and the baseball bat. So our Rule of Life on Vulnerability supports and encourages the inner adult as he or she hosts this essential and round-the-clock series of conversations.

When we are hurt, or in any kind of trouble, our reptilian brain takes the wheel, and we often say and do things that we later regret and that can make a bad situation worse. The chapters of our Vulnerability section tend to quiet the lizard-brain (and the inner children). We remember: "Oh. This bad stuff happens. Everyone remain calm. Let the adrenaline leave our bloodstream from that last, reactive pump, and in a while we can make level-headed decisions about the way forward."

Often, without these chapter reminders, we react rather than respond. We send a mean text or an angry or passive-aggressive email. But if every thirty days, we re-read, remind, and remember these love letters to ourselves, we will self-coach into the adult role and quiet the three children inside of us.

As I write my chapters on Vulnerability, Pia Mellody and others remind me that when I am wounded, I am tempted to wound back. And I must not. It will only feel good for about eight seconds. Maybe nine.

Break the cycle right now. Your anger does not give you the right to hurt people; your grief isn't license to pull away and disengage. Break the cycle, and you have a chance at a happy life. As a side note: If your parents were not great parents, then this inner work is all the more important. Your inner children need all the help they can get!

Our bodies feel pain as a warning. So do our minds, hearts, and souls. Feelings of grief, fear, and rage are red flags— warnings of pain. These chapters on Vulnerability can help train us to recognize warning signs and to understand pain as a guide in navigating this sometimes frightening life. It is better to consider pain, look it in the eye, and say: "I am not running. I will not hide. So tell me what I need to know." Then we can move on in stability.

A Word of Encouragement

This section can be hard to write. Or it can be so frothing around inside you that words sluice out as from a fire hydrant. Just thinking about our vulnerability, going to these places, can be difficult, and many are not used to sitting and thinking about vulnerability. We turn away. We grab a candy bar or a scotch. We sit trying to look nonchalant as we click the channels of our TV. In short, we resist the intimacy of vulnerability. And what we know about resistance is that it will slow us down from the inside like a ship dropping anchor or skis hitting dirt.

This is where page margins can make a difference. After you decide what chapters you want to write for Vulnerability, write the titles at the top of looseleaf pages, then run dark ink or pencil lines from top to bottom, about two inches from the left and right sides of the paper. (If you are working on a computer, create three columns.) Write your chapters in the middle of the page. Whenever you face writer's block or resistance, use the columns on the right and left to write key words that come to mind when you think of that particular chapter.

Let's say you want to write a chapter on suffering, but just thinking about suffering shuts you down, sending you in search of your addiction of choice for relief. Instead, move your pen (or cursor) to the columns and write some key words. This can help ease you into the topic of suffering word by word without having to actually deal with hard memories or write full sentences and paragraphs.

My column words for a suffering chapter might include: Pema Chödrön (a teacher of mine on suffering)/ Prague (I was hit by a train there, ouch)/ taste (I lost all taste when I was hit by that train…and I used to love food!)/ Tuffy (my first dog and my first experience of death)/ abandonment (my parents were…good at other things)/ and appendix surgery (the first searing pain I remember feeling).

The other suggestion for writing the chapters on Vulnerability is that you might need to chat with a close friend, spiritual director, or therapist. When I was first learning to ride a bicycle, my dad had to push it from behind to get me going. Going from stationary to hurtling down the street on a few bars of metal seemed crazy to me. I needed a shove. I needed one on a sled too. And on the diving board.

By sitting with someone who knows you well, you can get the help (push) you need to start addressing Vulnerability.

Chapter Suggestions

Suffering

You have experienced suffering. We all have. Suffering needs a chapter in our Rule because the process of writing and thinking about it, as well as the remembering each month, will remind us that suffering happens, that it is survivable and can produce growth. Furthermore, suffering need not—is best not—managed alone.

I turn to my chapter on suffering not only during its regular place in the monthly reading cycle but also throughout the month. Unlike others, reading this chapter more often than once a month provides a poignant and important reminder about the vulnerability of suffering.

Writing this chapter requires deep reflection: *How shall I greet suffering? From where will I find help?*

Fear

Fear poisons peace. There will always be fear, but how we meet fear is what determines how we respond or react. God knows that we are particularly prone to fear: Some form of "do not be afraid" is written in scripture more than 350 times!

So do not fear, for I am with you; do not be dismayed, for I am your God. I will strengthen you and help you; I will uphold you with my righteous right hand. —Isaiah 41:10

My chapter on fear acknowledges my typical response. When I am afraid, I move into fight-or-flight mode. But my Rule offers me monthly coaching in staying present, looking fear directly in the face, staring it down like the bully on the schoolyard, and then going for a nice long walk.

Your chapter on fear may remind you to stare fears down also. Perhaps you are like many people who feel the rush of emotions in a moment of fear: You want to attack and dominate one moment, and the next, you are tempted to collapse and curl up in a ball. Do neither. Stand firm and look fear in the eyes. Reject fear in favor of peacefulness.

Most of the fear I hear from people is about their worry for the future: *Will I be okay? Will I have enough money? How (and when) will I die?* Use your chapter to coach yourself into calm and away from worry. Your Rule will turn the lights on for you, but only you can choose not to be afraid. This chapter will coach you in fearlessness.

Uncertainty

One thing is certain: Nothing remains the same, everything will change, and life is full of uncertainties. We so cling to the security of certainty that we can miss wonderful opportunities at the edges of our lives. A chapter in our Rule of Life on uncertainty is a regular coach to us to greet the changes and chances of our lives with a gentle bow, not a punch in the eye.

And can any of you, by worrying, add a single hour to your span of life?—Matthew 6:27

I need a Rule of Life with a chapter on uncertainty because my chapter on fear is constantly tapping me on the shoulder and asking questions that the chapter on uncertainty is, needless to say, loathe to answer with any, well, certainty. Raising my tolerance for uncertainty is the hardest heavy lifting I have had to do in my life—and some of the best.

I often remember the words of one of my Buddhist teachers, Pema Chödrön: "As human beings, not only do we seek resolution, but we also feel that we deserve resolution. However, not only do we not deserve resolution, we suffer from resolution. We don't deserve resolution; we deserve something better than that. We deserve our birthright, which is the middle way, an open state of mind that can relax with paradox and ambiguity" (*When Things Fall Apart: Heart Advice for Difficult Times*).

Financial systems will fail us. Friendships will wither and sometimes even curdle. A vacation may turn into a terrible loss. A lover may leave. What seems like a great job or marriage or house may turn into a disaster as might a sunny day. And just as likely, a lottery ticket may be a winner, a date may become a seven-decade love affair, a wrong turn in the car may take you to a more beautiful place than the intended destination. Uncertainty works both ways. Your Rule of Life coaches you into a tolerance for uncertainty by reminding you to welcome it, not fight it.

In life—and in the church—too many are too sure of too much. My prayer is not that I am able to be certain, but that the people I love will share courage with me in our uncertainty. I pray that my Rule will coach me in being open to everything, judging nothing. As author Byron Katie says, "Love what is."

Grief and Loss

Grief and loss are equal opportunity life invaders. We may lose a job or accidentally break a favorite bowl (which, I might add, happened to me seconds before writing these words). We may lose a friend to death or a marriage to a thousand cuts. One wrong investment can be a disaster for a retired couple. After being a foodie all of my life, a train accident took my ability to taste and smell. For loss, grief holds the tray like an aged, sad butler.

A chapter on grief and loss can offer helpful encouragement, reminding us that both are normal parts of life, better faced than ignored, and usually temporary. Your chapter on loss and grief will be a great comfort to you when you come upon it in your cycle of chapter readings because it will remind you that grief and loss are survivable. My chapter on loss soothes me like a therapist and comforts me like a mother. My chapter on loss and grief says: "Sweet one, this happens. How you feel is normal. Go ahead and weep. Then do the laundry."

Write about how you best heal from grief and loss. Coach yourself so that when in grief and loss, you know what to do to climb out of the hole, and you know what you need from God, from friends, and from yourself (self care, rest, caution around food and alcohol, etc.) that will get you back on your feet and on your cheerful way again.

Envy

Envy makes us vulnerable to misplaced desire. Whenever I see something I want, I ask myself: Is this truly something I want or is it is simply a symbol of a deeper need or desire? Indeed, a Rule of Life offers guardrails so that we do not grab and collect every sparkly thing we see. A chapter on envy coaches us on things like binge shopping, television with commercials, spontaneous purchases, shopping for the power rush, and holding self-esteem in the face of the media. One of the self-coachings in my own Rule is this: I ask myself to wait twenty-four hours before making the purchase of something for which I am not shopping, something I just see along the way. My rule asks me to take great care when buying things and never to spontaneously make a purchase.

Envy runs our economy. Envy sells things. It takes perfectly wonderful people and sours, embitters, and wizens them by using insecurities to coax them to want, crave, and long for things, people, jobs, titles, bodies, and a whole host of symbols that indicate glamour and prestige.

We all need some self-coaching in our Rule to help us remember to choose to be centered, peaceful human beings rather than possession mongers. On any given day, we may choose peace over materialism, but to do so requires that we pursue a countercultural way of life.

Next Steps

How we embrace vulnerability as human beings with bodies that are soft and feelings that can easily bruise is vitally important. Our Rule coaches us so that when we face vulnerability, we have been training long enough that we are ready. Jesus did this work through silence in the mountains, in gardens, and with the Father but also through spending time with friends in an upper room and on the beach. We know the pain of our vulnerability, and we know that God has chosen vulnerability as the hallmark of saving grace through Christ's willing self-offering. So we pray to God who knows, physically, viscerally, of what we speak. God understands what we ask and need. My chapters around the vulnerability of life remind me that I am not alone and that there are tools and actions that can be of great help.

At this point you might want to go to your journal or to a set of Post-it notes to write out a list of vulnerability chapters that make sense to you. Perhaps you need to change the section title from Vulnerability to some other word that seems right to you, such as Wounds and Losses or Responding to Life or When Bad Things Happen. There are lots of way to target the issue.

Be creative, but stay focused. Beware of avoiding the hard stuff. Name the painful, loss-filled realities of life and deal with them in the writing of your Rule. Otherwise, you will end up with a collection of pious greeting-card quotations. It will not be the Rule of Life that you need—or that God wants for you.

Study Questions for Draft Chapters

Suffering

- What do scripture, great writers, and big thinkers say about suffering? Do these quotes help by prodding you into deeper thought? Is there a particular quotation that you might want to use as a guide or reminder?
- How has your suffering contributed to your goodness, strength, and resilience? How might you remind yourself that suffering can form and deepen us?
- If you were standing with yourself, what would you say to encourage yourself on the topic of suffering? Knowing the inevitability of suffering, what might you say to your non-suffering self?

- Who do you know who has suffered deeply and returned from those valleys with wisdom and peace? Consider calling or visiting them and asking them to offer words of support and encouragement that you might use in your chapter.
- What has it felt like to be on the other side of suffering? What words do you have for yourself that will encourage you to keep going, take one more step, plan one more section of the day?

Fear

- Where do you hold your fear? What part of your body holds fear? Which people calm your fears? How can you remind yourself of the things you can do to reduce your fears?
- How can you remind yourself of the work you do when in the midst of anxious thoughts? Who would you be without your fears?
- Can you write briefly about a time when you were in great fear only to find that the fears were entirely unwarranted? How can you coach your future self to resist fear?
- What religious rituals help mitigate your fears? How can you remind yourself of those so that when you are afraid, you know where to turn?
- Many people awaken in the middle of the night with terrible fears. If you struggle with insomnia and related fears, what can you do to encourage sleeping deeply? These might include limiting computer and television time or alcohol and caffeine intake.
- What is your advice to yourself regarding fears? How might you encourage yourself?

Uncertainty

- What troubles you about uncertainty? What gives you hope to face uncertainty?
- Who do you know who deals well with uncertainty? Consider talking to or emailing them to learn about self-care and self-coaching, so you can add it to your own chapter on uncertainty.
- What would it take to imagine joy and delight emerging from uncertainty? How can you hold uncertainty without teetering and falling into fear?
- What happens when you overfunction and try to avoid uncertainty?
- What have great minds written about uncertainty?
- What would it take for you to face uncertainty with the vulnerability of open hands and a willing heart, to welcome, rather than fight, what is and what might be?

Grief and Loss

- Where have you experienced grief and loss in your life? How do you best move from grief and loss into peace?
- What words of encouragement do you have for yourself as you imagine dealing with grief and loss? How can you coach yourself in the kind of self-care needed when experiencing grief and loss?
- What do well-regarded writers, theologians, scholars, mystics, prophets, and authors say about grief and loss? What is in the mouths of the characters of fiction with regard to grief and loss? Think of your favorite writers and run an internet search of their names with the word "grief" and then with the word "loss." What do they say that you find encouraging and that you might include in your chapter?

- Many times, grief and loss come to us in small doses, easily disregarded. What do you need to say to yourself that reminds you to care gently for your small losses? Do you need to tell your story? See a counselor? Get a two-hour massage? Write your vision for what you need to heal.

Envy

- How does envy manifest in your life? Does it show you what you desire? Do you want the thing or person or do you want something deeper? Do you want a new coat or do you want to feel beautiful? Do you want a new car or do you want to be impressive?
- What triggers envy in your life? Is it visual? Is it touch-based? Does your envy focus more on people who have the things you want, the status that things bring, or the power you wish you had? Are you vulnerable to the envy of youth, beauty, or giftedness?
- How do your own insecurities inform the things you want and desire? What envies seem to show up frequently for you? How might you manage those recurring themes?
- What helps you move out of envy? Is it best to avoid commercials, throw away catalogs, stay off the web, or avoid certain gatherings? Do you need to encourage yourself to make only planned purchases? How would this chapter interface with your chapter on money or possessions?
- What do others say about envy in their lives? What do authors and novel characters and great thinkers say about envy? When you read these quotes, can you see how your truth is amplified by some of their truth?

Closing Prayers

Here are some prayers I have written to end my chapters on
Vulnerability. I go to these prayers when my own words fail
me, which happens in the section on Vulnerability more than
any other section.

A Prayer for Suffering

*God who suffered, hear me. Hear all of us who suffer at
times. Hear us cry out. Hear our pain and confusion, our
disappointment and our surprise. Help me to examine my
life so that I look directly at pain and have some chance of
lessening my own suffering by answering pain's questions.
And when I suffer at the hands of nature, body, or ego, give to
me the peace that inclines me to look for you in the darkness,
seeking your presence in the rivers in which I stand, rivers
within which you also stand. Amen.*

A Prayer When in Fear

*Over and over again, you call us to not be afraid. Be present
with us as a mother hen broods over her chicks and tucks them
under her wings. When fires of life rage, keep your wings over
us, and those we love, and over every sentient being. Pour cool
water on the fires of our fears, dousing flames and cooling the
embers that are ready to reignite with the slightest provocation.
Sit with us in the third watch, that night transition when we are
at our weakest. Remind us that peace is a choice. Amen.*

A Prayer for Living with Uncertainty

*Everything changes, and life undulates like the waters of an
ocean, churning, circulating, swirling in constant change.
Nothing stays the same and yet we humans are designed
for some stability. Lord God, grant us peace in the midst of
uncertainty. Blow 'round us, Holy Spirit, with soothing summer*

winds when change-terror invades our soul with chills. Help us to greet all change with an assurance of your presence with us. Remind us of the spiritual practices that ground us, even when the winds of change swirl around us. And grant us peace that passes all understanding. Amen.

A Prayer When in Grief and Loss
God of all mercy, be present in our grief and loss and hold us in the hollow of your hand. Hear us when we cry out to you in our grief and wipe every tear from our eyes when what we love or want or need is taken from us. When our gut feels empty and no one sits with us in our sadness, send your Holy Spirit to comfort and restore us. Help us to remember that Easter always follows Lent and the sun always rises after darkness. Whisper into grief that all shall be well, that all things shall be well, and that all manner of things shall be well. Amen.

A Prayer When in Envy
It is said that the eyes are a lamp unto the soul, and it is with our eyes that we see so many things and are persuaded by advertising to want them. Bombarded by the internet, television, billboards, bench-backs, and newspaper ads, we allow these images to play on our deepest fears and insecurities, creating needs where they don't exist and wants that distract us from our enough. Form us in your image that we may stand firm against the winds of envy and stand surefooted in your love. Amen.

Chapter 9

On Body

We emerge from Vulnerability to a section on the Body,
this most vulnerable mass of flesh and bone that hosts the
darknesses and vulnerabilities we have been considering.
At the same time, the body is the means by which we hear
Mozart, feel the lamb's ear, smell lavender, taste butter, and
feel the touch of a friend or lover.

We will look at our mortality and how aspects of it invite the
channeling of passions and energies, choices and longings,
realities and even failures. The body is the vessel that carries
us around, and so it is a temple and lantern that bears Christ's
light to others. Let us consider the body and its need for a
Rule of Life, one that encourages and gathers its boundaries,
comforts its limitations, and yet not for a moment diminishes
its joys and pleasures.

Our body is what we inhabit on this planet. It enables
connection to people, food, work, and land. Our body is a
miracle of muscles, blood vessels, nerves, brain cells, and
calcium covered by a thin-skin boundary full of feelings. Yes,
our body can sicken, and yet that our body is so often well is
amazing to me. Our body allows for and enables delights of

many kinds and is a precious possession of each human. We get only one.

Our body can also feel terrible pain, experience exhaustion, and create layers of fat that separate us from the planet. Many of us care more for our cars than we do for our bodies; we carry our computers with more caution than we do our brain and the viruses to which we expose it.

In our body is stardust and into our nostrils we breathe dust. Our secretions may hold pieces of pyramids, the blood of a Roman soldier, the skin flake of a British royal, the rice dust from a Hong Kong street vendor, or a floating flake from the true cross. Matter circles. It does not stay in a reliquary easily or for long. Matter floats. Matter is ingested, and matter becomes part of other matter. God became matter—body—as a way to connect with humanity. Jesus' cells were replaced five times over, billions of bits and pieces floating into air and water that first century. They are still floating here and there, even today, perhaps floating down into the milk of my morning cereal while I am busy getting the coffee.

It is breathtaking to consider how our body works, with its 37 trillion cells generating, dying, and being replaced every seven years. It is hard to imagine, without medical training, the 60,000 miles of blood vessels in our body and their ability to work correctly. My brain does not understand how its brain-self works, and yet it seems able to direct my body, store information, calculate problems, and consider its thoughts while hosting sexuality, downloading God's still small voice, processing food, dreaming, holding a friend's hand, and appreciating the beauty of a red leaf.

Our human brain receives 11 million messages each second. The only way for our brains to manage is to attend consciously to about forty messages at a time. And on bad days, we can manage even less. Most of these messages are from within our body and yet, because they are not sensed as external threats, they are managed with little or no background thought processes.

But 11 million messages! Perhaps our gratitude for this one life we have been given can be best expressed by how we attend to our body. This section in our Rule of Life on Body can help us to treat our bodies with the care they deserve, for a Rule is about living carefully and mindfully.

My Rule of Life chapters on the Body are very tender—kind even. I invite you to be tender with your self as well. Issues with our bodies and how we relate to them can be fraught. Be gentle but honest: In what ways can you care for your body so that it might be the vessel God intends? As a potter, my clay runs through my hands as the wheel spins beneath it. As a spiritual person, my life runs through my Rule and the days spin beneath it. Let the Potter make you into the vessel you both choose together.

Chapter Suggestions

Health

The Bible's words about my body being a temple sounded like a platitude when I was younger. But after a half-century of life, I find my aching self willing and able to care for my body and its health.

My Rule of Life chapter on health is a regular and helpful reminder of what is important in life about having and caring for a human body: mine, this one typing right now. After the

Victorian-workhouse experience of monastic life, I have made new vows to have comfortable chairs for this long body and to do the math daily, relentlessly, regarding sleep. I am unwilling to give myself less than an eight-hour window for sleep, needed or not.

My health chapter includes a section about alarm clocks too. They are for mornings when I have a flight to catch, but generally I keep them turned off. I listen to books to go to sleep in a room intentionally darkened one hour before my intended sleep. I drink no caffeine of any kind after mid-morning no matter how tired I feel. I give myself permission to nap more and with less guilt, and I keep scented oils with which to rub down my body on the eve of my sabbath day as a ritual reminder that my body has great value, does me very great service on this planet, and will one day be anointed for death. Let your Rule of Life celebrate life, not scold it. The Rule is not a list of don'ts. The Rule is a channeling of joy as much as it is a reminder of care. The Rule is invitatory, inviting you to remember and live your longings.

Write your Rule's chapter on health with your body in mind. Do not use the chapter to chastise your body, its shape, its fatigue, or its weaknesses. Use the chapter to remind yourself about what you want for your body.

Use your chapter to remind yourself what your body enjoys and what limitations make it feel better. If you have trouble limiting alcohol, late-night working sessions, or food, then this is a chapter in which to address those longings.

Your chapter on health may need a paragraph or phrase on an illness you need to manage, reminding you of ways you need to live and choices you need to make to live a healthy life in its context. Your chapter may need to offer self-coaching on some things you enjoy for good health, such as vitamins, yoga, exercise, stretching, sunlight, walking, or sex.

If you are not sure how to begin, simply make a list of key words that you associate with your body's health, weaknesses, and wellness, then reorder the words into an outline. Write through the outline using each word in a sentence or two. As I mentioned before, this list may go easily into the margins of the page.

Play

You may wonder why I list play as a primary suggestion for a chapter in a Rule of Life. Science has proven, and psychology asserts, that play is crucial to the wellness of the human mind and body. Play helps creativity, teaches capacity, prompts ingenuity, and recycles repressed feelings. When I die, I will wish I had played more. My Rule encourages it every few weeks when I read this chapter to myself. Look at my calendar, and you will see that the seven days after I read my chapter on play are full of play appointments I have made for myself. Remember to play.

In the psalms, God laughs when the prideful are, well, prideful. In Ecclesiastes, there are times set aside for a myriad of things: building, keeping, tearing down, singing, dancing, weeping, and, yes, laughing. I believe in a human Jesus as much as a divine Jesus, and so I allow, rather robustly, for Jesus to have played from birth to death. Even laughed.

What is play for you now? Think about your life and how play shows up for you. Is it a day in a museum, time in a pottery class, an afternoon with a mystery or thriller under a tree, a beer and some wings with a friend, a great movie, a board or card game with friends, a bath with a lover, an amusement park, or time with your grandchildren? What delights you? Have you forgotten the list? Did you ever give yourself permission to have a list?

Use this chapter in your Rule to coach yourself—to remind yourself—of play and of how you like to play. And in the margins of the page, occasionally write down new forms of play as you notice them. Later, rewrite your chapter to include these types of play.

Home

Home means different things to different people. Some of my friends say that home is the people we love. Other friends describe a building in which we feel safe, dry, and fed. I agree with my friends.

I remember that fateful moment when, sitting in my monk's habit on a discernment of vows retreat, my spiritual director said simply, "What do you want?" The question disarmed me since I expected a question more like: "What is God calling you to do with your life as a monk?" Immediately I answered the question: "I want to have my dining room table back. I want my friends around it, and I want the candles to burn all the way down while we eat four or five courses in as many hours, guts busting with laughter. I want a black Lab dog, and I want a home with a wood stove."

I was stunned. I had no idea those longings were so strong in me. I was on the edge of my seat, leaning forward. My voice had been so loud there seemed to have been an echo. My spiritual director responded, gently smiling as if to suppress a laugh, "Then go do that! Go do that! LIVE. Make a home."

I experienced tremendous grief at leaving the cloistered life, but I knew what I wanted. I wanted a home: safe, kind, gentle, warm. And the monastery was not a home for me.

You may be reading this book in your home. Look around it. Love it. Appreciate its gorgeous sanctuary by writing a chapter of your Rule on home. It is in our homes that we are the midwives of our life. God pitches God's tent among us, through Jesus who will lead us home.

In this chapter you will want to remind yourself of your own longings and hopes for home, however you define it. You may want reminders of how you want to use your home: in hospitality, in solitude, for friendship, for study or rest, and for family. You may want to remind yourself of the importance of home for keeping sabbath and so, as is often the case, your chapter on home will overlap with other chapters such as family, friendship, sabbath, and silence.

Home is a wonderful place for life and love, but it can also be a safe place in which suffering is held safe and slowly healed. A place for solitude, home is also a place of sanctuary in which doorbell and phones are only answered if and as I choose. The street approach to my home in Denver was one massive white wall with a wrought iron gate. When my friend saw it, he exclaimed: "It's a tiny, two-room monastery!" There were no windows to the street and no house door on the street. The gate was to a secret high-walled garden. The house was glass and ran alongside the garden.

In a society in which there is so much doing and so little being, my Rule on home includes my observations on my own boundaries. For example, my cell phone is not kept in my home on a sabbath day. I keep it in the car in order to assure myself of some silence and deep rest. I have a list of my friends in a document on my computer desktop called "The Garden" (an allusion to the need for friendship's curating, watering, pruning, planting, removal, and growth), and my Rule expresses my desire to have my home filled with friends.

If you want to simplify your home—declutter it, keep it clean, re-orient possessions—then write about that longing in your Rule to serve as a monthly reminder. My Rule, for example, reminds me not to store things. I keep only the things I use daily.

Rather than finding a home and then realizing my Rule did not fit the house, I read my Rule and then find and decorate my house to fit my Rule—my written, curated longings for my life. By choosing a house based on my Rule, I am living my longed-for life.

Intimacy, Touch, and Sex

My brain confuses hunger and thirst. If I drink water and wait fifteen minutes, I am less hungry because I had my signals crossed. I think sex and touch work the same way. When we think we want sex, we are often simply craving touch or connection. Your Rule of Life should remind you of your longings for sex and intimacy. Your Rule is a set of longings and reminders, so they may not always be fulfilled. Your Rule is a reminder of hopes.

Intimacy is perhaps more important to write about to yourself than even touch and sex, since connection is so important for the human psyche. Linked to your other Rule chapters on friendship or perhaps marriage, intimacy needs to be part of your Rule of Life so that you are reminded of your need to connect to others. In my Rule are references to issues that orbit intimacy, such as trust, forgiveness, the scheduling of time with friends, and intimate conversations that I especially need in times of trouble. As I read my chapter on intimacy every few weeks, I am forced to ask myself: "Will a massage or holding a friend's hand feed my need for touch? Am I making time for friends? Am I choosing the right friends? When was the last time I called a friend and made fun plans?" By reading my chapter and then asking these questions, I am living the life I want instead of mindlessly letting days slip by, made up solely of work and sleep.

We each have two fences between us and other people, their fence and ours. They are responsible for where their fence is, and I am responsible for where mine is. Healthy boundaries are important, and so intimacy with different people will be more or less dependent on where you place your fence with them. My Rule of Life reminds me of this monthly, and so there is always an occasion to check my "relationship fences," just like ranchers check their cattle fences.

Intimacy, touch, and sex are important to human happiness. The simple act of taking the time to ask yourself what you think of them will transform your self-understanding, and the writing down of those thoughts into a Rule of Life will give you license to enjoy life but with boundaries.

Next Steps

If you are living life without a partner (widowed, divorced, solitary, separated) or without one who is able to provide you with intimacy (and not all partners are able), then your Rule may be a loving reminder to you to find intimacy where and as you can. Find intimacy that remains within the boundaries of your morals and your Rule (friendship, touch, weekends with close friends, hand holding, etc.) and state to yourself what those boundaries are so that you remember intimacy rightly, since biology will sometimes interfere with your choice making. If and when you need to change your views on intimacy, you may simply edit your Rule.

If you are a person currently with a spouse or partner, your Rule may remind you of the vows you have taken and the need to explore intimacy and sex within these parameters. If you anesthetize your pain with casual sex or visual stimulation such as pornography, then you will want to gently remind yourself in your Rule that, like alcohol, shopping, and food, our drugs of choice may dull the dark but do not eradicate it. And of course when we dull the dark, we dull the light as well. When we pollute our bodies, we live half-lives. Our Rule coaches us to live full, honest lives, with healthy integrity.

Our body is not only a temple, it is also a vehicle for getting around. Our body is important, needing gentle kindness, needing protection from addictions and external threats. So chapters on the body including health, play, and home, as well as intimacy, touch, and sex, are very important elements of your Rule. You may have others such as massage if that is important to you, diet if eating is an issue, or physical therapy, if your body needs that work to regain its strength. You may also include these topics (and others) as sentences or paragraphs within your current health chapter. Finally, try not to be squeamish about drafting this section on Body. My dad always told me never to write down anything I would not feel comfortable seeing on the front page of the *New York Times*. And I get that. But when it comes to my Rule of Life, I do not need it to be some great work of spiritual piety that sets me up for posterity as a kind of saint. I am happy to exchange piety for goodness. My Rule of Life is a private document used only by me.

Of all the sections, my chapter on Body is the most visceral. Other sections can get very philosophical, spiritual, or aspirational. But the chapters on Body deal with decisions that can cause great delight or great harm, to me and to others. Take care to be honest and clear with yourself. You have only one body and only for a short time. Care for it tenderly.

Study Questions for Draft Chapters

Health

- What is your vision for the physical health of your life?
- What contributes to your physical well-being?
- What do you know about what you put into your body? What is good and what is bad?
- What do you enjoy that soothes your body? (baths, massages, oiled skin, foot massages, hand massages, the touch of a friend, certain music, smells, naps, a dark room, a gentle book, or dietary decisions.) What is your self-coaching about these things?
- What harms your body's well-being and well-feeling? Harmful items might include late-night drinks, caffeine, overwork, acidic foods, bad shoes, late-night television, late-night internet surfing, or overscheduling. What is your Rule about these things? How would you coach yourself to reduce these things for a healthier life?

Play

- Why do you think play is important in a human's life? What about in your human life?
- What have others said of the benefits of play?
- What needs to happen in your life to allow for or encourage play? Options might include rest, sleep, time, managing work addiction, taking yourself less seriously, amusement park visits, fun activities on vacations, game night with friends, or hobbies such as doodling, pottery, or cooking.
- What would you need to risk in order to play as much as would be good for you?
- What things are counterfeit versions of play, things you used to consider play but now know are bad for your body, mind, or soul? How might you replace them with more healthy forms of play? How would you coach yourself in that exchange?

Home

- What is your vision of home? How may you make a home for yourself?
- What kind of land or setting is best for your home?
- What personality traits, values, anxieties, annoyances, or delights do you want for your home?
- What things do you enjoy in your home? I want a good crockpot, a fireplace, and a recliner. What are your home priorities for rooms? Why have a home with rooms you do not use? Let your Rule direct the choice of your home.
- If you are like many, you might want a coaching paragraph or sentence in your Rule about storage. You

may want to set some boundaries like: "If an item is stored for more than a year without being touched, it is sold or given away." I love Marie Kondo's work on tidying up. She touches and asks each thing in her home if it gives her joy. If not, it leaves the home.

- How does your home create a safe and soothing place for rest, play, intimacy, eating, study, conversation, hospitality, and prayer? What barriers to your longings for home exist in your current home? What do you need to do about that to make changes? Is where you live a home or a living space?

Intimacy, Touch, and Sex

- What are your longings for intimacy in your life? What provides you with the intimacy you need for survival and thriving, and what tends to block, counterfeit, or erode intimacy in your life? What different kinds of intimacy do you value? Remind yourself in your Rule.
- What is the level and kind of intimacy for this time in your life right now? How might you craft a life with more intimacy? How have you confused sex and intimacy? How might you mitigate against those confusions?
- How do you get the touch you need in your life? What anxieties about touch exist for you and how might those be healed? Has touch become a difficult thing for you because of abuse, abandonment, or boundary violations? How might you heal from that fear?
- What needs to happen in your life on a day-to-day basis that will allow for more touch or intimacy in your life?

- Is your sex life a place of health and renewal? What needs to change in your life so that you have the kind of sex life that you want?
- If your life is celibate through religious vows, disease, advanced age, memories of sexual abuse, or some other blocking issue that prevents you from having sex with others, what do you need to do to take care of yourself? If anxiety about sex is bound up with spiritual or theological issues, what do you need to do to get help?

Closing Prayers

A Prayer for Health

You are a God who became human in order to have a body that might better invite connection with your people. I have a body, and I want to care for it gently. When I push it too hard, guide me to gentleness. When I abuse my body with chemicals or unhealthy relationships, whisper to my inner teenager that you love me and will not let me harm myself. Give me the self-regard for my wellness that inclines me to eat carefully and sleep naturally and in peace. Amen.

A Prayer for Play

The platypus, the three-toed sloth, and the palate of colors among flowers and animals remind me of your playfulness, great God of the cosmos. You created 2,000 kinds of praying mantis alone, and you created humans with humor and ticklish parts of the body. When we are frightened or grief-stricken, bring into our lives people whose playfulness storms our gates and softens our hearts. Amen.

A Prayer for Home

*Our home is in you, Creator of the cosmos. My body needs
a home in order to find safety, rest, and the opportunity for
connections with humans and companion animals. Grant
me a home in which I might rest, cook, eat, sleep, and play.
When it is possible, may I create a beautiful home and keep it
beautiful. Let my home be a place of sanctuary for me and for
those I love. And at my last awakening, may I, and all sentient
beings, enter a new home prepared for us, who love you and
whom you love.* Amen.

A Prayer for Intimacy, Touch, and Sex

*You, God of the jungles and oceans, the forests and animal
kingdoms, create beings that live and procreate. Your life in
the Trinity is generative of love, one to the other in a loop-de-
loop of dynamic energy. You created touch and sensuality,
and you blessed it all with joy. Grant us the freedom to enjoy
our bodies in safe and healthy ways. When we are insecure,
grant us confidence, and when we misuse sexuality, intimacy,
or touch, grant to us an awareness of the beauty and value of
ordered, playful lives.* Amen.

Chapter 10

On Thought

In our section on Listening, we looked at our relationship with God. How do we listen so that God informs our lives? Our section on Being considered how we relate to the life and people around us, how we love, create, relate, work, and rest. Then we explored Vulnerability—what keeps us well, unafraid, and aware of our pain but not overcome by it. We considered our Body, examining ways to take care of and inhabit our bodies with mindfulness.

In this section, we will think about Thought. What goes on in our thoughts has an impact on our perception of every other topic in this book. We think about God and our lives, bodies, and vulnerabilities, and process these ideas through a computer we call "thought."

We consider our thoughts so that we are not beaten about by the winds of various messages emanating from within and from outside us. The noise inside and outside of us can be damaging if it is not carefully curated. Otherwise, we may find ourselves in a hurricane of thoughts, which make it difficult to live a centered, well-focused life. You and I are the only ones who can do that curating for ourselves.

Chapter Suggestions

Discernment and Discretion

As adults, we make about 35,000 choices per day. Some choices are impulsive. Some are a matter of compliance or delegation, while others are based in either avoidance or deflection. Some are high stakes like what job to take, whom to marry, and where to live. Many of our choices are of smaller consequence: what to order for dinner or which outfit to wear.

Some decisions require a high emotional and spiritual intelligence. They involve balancing, prioritizing, and reflecting. These decisions engage discernment. Discernment is the ancient spiritual discipline of carefully considering thoughts and prayers about a specific issue in the context of a belief that God exists and has an opinion about the outcome. Discernment is predicated on the expectation that God has hopes and longings for the life we live and the way our life fits in with the choices made by the billions of other people on the planet.

The Latin word *discretio* includes both discernment and the second part of our chapter title, discretion. Discernment asks about our "yes." Discretion asks about the "no."

My chapter on discernment and discretion has served me well over the years, reminding me that choice-making is important and that God is active and present, constantly using people, experiences, and scripture to encourage me toward some choices and away from others. When I read the chapter on discernment in my own Rule, I am re-minded, re-self-coached that choices matter and that there is a process involved in making good choices.

Here is how I move through the process of discernment and discretion:

- I try to make a choice in a time of peace in my life.
- I state the possible choice (i.e., taking a new job in Minnesota).
- I divide a piece of paper into four columns. In two columns, over a few days or weeks, I make lists of the pros and cons of the choice. Then in the other two columns, I make lists of the pros of not making the choice and the cons of not making the choice. There should be four columns in total.
- Over a few days or weeks, I strike through the silly ones with a red pen.
- With a highlighter, I highlight the items I love and feel are good pros or strong cons. Then I test the list against what I am hearing in prayer, intellect, data, reason, and from people I love and trust.
- Over time, I make a choice based on the highlighted lists. Once I have made the choice, I evaluate whether it feels good or not in my gut. If it doesn't feel good and right, I begin again.
- I try not to be seduced by the wolf in lamb's clothing: I encourage you to make choices based on goodness, not piety, lust, greed, ego, or cravings.

Detachment

If discretion is the sister of discernment, then detachment is their crazy Aunt Mildred. The ancient practice of detachment can be difficult. A chapter in your Rule on detachment invites you to a spiritual practice that is well-known for the freedom it can enable in a human life, yet is often met with deep resistance.

This chapter in your Rule will be your self-coaching around letting go of things, situations, jobs, relationships, and even health and life. If we hold things lightly, then change is not so frightening or painful. When we white-knuckle our lives, over-identifying our egos with what we hold tightly, needless suffering occurs.

Detachment, even from something dearly beloved and something one is convinced one has earned or deserves, is a freeing spiritual practice. As we strive to live our best lives, we must also be able to detach and move on. Detachment means we live with open cool hands rather than sweaty, clenched fists. To live with detachment is to allow for the possibility that what happens in life is to be loved, rather than fought with. To live a life of healthy detachment is to be free in the realities of a changing body, life, and world.

Detachment makes moving on possible. It can also take serious courage to live this way, and it is a Rule we may often fail to accomplish. It is hard work but worth it.

Technology and Media

My Rule of Life has a short chapter on media and technology both because they play such a large role in our society and because I want some confinement and intentionality around them in my own life. I am not a Luddite, rejecting cell phones and television and complaining about the modern glare of the electric light bulb.

As I sit in restaurants, meetings, and even retreats, I see people constantly checking emails, texts, and news. We are, many of us, addicted to our technologies, and they become more deeply entrenched by the year as new toys come on the market. Soon eye glasses and windshields in driverless cars will flash texts and emails at us. Futurists say that in thirty years any pane of glass in our homes will, with the touch of a finger, become a computer screen. That's a lot of input.

Two things have exploded since the 1800s. One is the planet's population, and the other is the data we are digesting. Neither is tenable. For this chapter, we won't address the planet's population, but we can explore our relationship with technology. Given our collective tendency to be addicted to technology, I encourage you to consider intentional confinements around the use of technology and media. We humans need about twenty-five minutes to refocus after an interruption. Our cell phones alone will ping or buzz most of us about every eighteen minutes. This means that our ability to focus mentally, emotionally, and spiritually is waning at alarming speeds.

As you draft your chapter on this subject, try not to focus on scolding but rather on the invitation of the freedoms you can imagine from defining and confining technology and media. Your chapters are not here to dominate you like angry substitute teachers wagging bony fingers at you for misbehaving. Instead your chapters are invitations to a healthy, centered life and to all the joys that emerge from it.

Here are some of the items that form the outline of my chapter on technology and media:
- On sabbath days I never look at work emails or phone messages.
- My chapter reminds me never to look at my phone when speaking to or sitting with humans.
- I watch television that has no commercials, especially before Christmas when marketing is so seductive.

- I try to avoid any backlit screen (computer, television, iPhone, etc.) for one hour before sleep so that my brain is able to perceive night and duly respond.
- When surfing the internet I try to look at things that my closest and most-centered friends would consider appropriate.
- If I see something online that I want to buy, I wait twenty-four hours before making the purchase, in order to discern the need or want.

Study and Formation

The inner life is every bit as big a world as the planet on which we live. There is so much to see, do, and learn about, both inside us and outside!

Curiosity is a sacrament—or should be. It serves me well, and I think it is a reasonable way to respond to a God who has been so creative inside and outside our bodies. Curiosity fuels creativity, welcomes encounter, upends established prejudices, and heals wounded hearts. So I study, read, and seek the wisdom of the people who think great thoughts and write about them.

Yet best intentions to engage in study and formation often get edged out by the daily responsibilities of life. We need to get the garbage out, dog walked, house cleaned, bills paid, work done, shower taken, emails returned, meals shopped for, prepared, and eaten…the list goes on. So who has time for study? Who has time to be formed by the writings of great thinkers? Most days it is all I can do to tie my shoes and drive my car. How will I ever find the time to study the classics, watch interesting TED talks, watch valuable speakers on YouTube, or listen to the podcasts like "On Being" (my personal favorite)—all things that make me think bigger thoughts and live a better, more open and curious life?

Well, the answer lies in the little word "find." The truth is that unless I am occasionally reminded to study and inquire, by reading this chapter, I will not find the time for study and formation. But when I read this chapter of my Rule, I am reminded, coached, and encouraged. "Oh, that's right!" I say to myself, "I love to be curious. I love to learn. I love to hear what great thinkers think!" As I reread my chapter on study and formation, I remember and reattach myself to my longing to be informed and formed. When I remember this desire for curiosity, I stop trying to *find* the time and commit to *making* the time for study.

What I notice about myself is that I make time for things that are important, and I find time for everything else. It's like money. I make money because finding money does not actually pay the bills. This chapter reminds me to make time for study and for the formation that makes me less pious and more kind. Jesus and his followers listened to scripture and discussed it, but they did not have the competition of television, movies, and complex possessions. So we need a chapter on study to give ourselves permission to learn, read, and think about our lives. Living a life without curiosity and study seems like a contract with isolation.

Failure

Yeah. I know. Can't we skip this one? This chapter can seem, at first, to be a total bummer. But we need to be honest: Failure will come from time to time. Our egos do not like to even host the possibility of failure, and many of us work hard to avoid the hint of failure in our lives. I personally am great at naming other people's failures (much to their annoyance), but I am much less willing to name and accept my own.

The storied British leader Winston Churchill said that "success is stumbling from failure to failure with no loss of enthusiasm," and I tend to agree. Considering failure is not shame-based but an opportunity for learning. Failure is a class in what my spiritual director used to call "Jesus' little school."

Of course, failure can be painful. It can inspire shame, guilt, loss, and second-guessing of our ability or intellect. But after a great fall—and once we have given ourselves some time to wallow in the reality of our failure—this chapter reminds us to summon the courage to get up, brush ourselves off, and spray some spiritual, relational, psychological, or even physical equivalent of Bactine on our scraped-up selves. It is time for a bandage and a march into the future with the new learnings from our old fall.

Unfortunately this is not always our response. All too often we reach for a form of self-anesthesia to dull the pain of the failure, and ultimately ignore it, pretending it did not happen. We fail during a conversation by spouting a mean comment and then reach for the TV remote so that there is no silence in which to feel the guilt of a terrible thing spoken. We send a mean email and then quickly surf the internet for a sweater or a new gadget so as not to think about what we just sent. We poison relationships and then reach for a new relationship to soothe our anxious conscience.

When we can see that failure, like change, is a regular, if occasionally unwelcome, reality, we can make friends with it as an agent of formation and conversion. American novelist Truman Capote sums this up: "Failure is the condiment that gives success its flavor." Failure teaches us who we are, but if we do not face our failures then they become who we are, the food rather than the flavor.

My chapter on failure is, like the rest of them, a love letter by me, to me, and from both me and God. It says to me some mornings when it shows up in the rotation: "Sweet one, it's okay. Yes. You just failed. Lay there a bit before you get up. You are not alone. I am here. Let me stroke your hair and kiss that forehead of yours. I know. It hurts. It does. But a little cleaning up and some antibiotic, and you will be walking again and then, running. You ache right now but that will fade." And after a little time of recovery, that still, small voice that I attribute to God asks, as gently as the afternoon sun on a rose petal, "So... sweet one...what did you learn?"

We need our chapter on failure to remind us that we will fail, that we will heal, and that we will learn.

Next Steps

I tend to let thoughts stampede through my brain like a thousand bulls through a Spanish town, crushing ideas, stomping on hopes, galloping over tender sprouts of ideas. Overcaffeinated, exhausted, and constantly on the lookout for danger around every corner, many of us are so busy being afraid that we don't leave space for other thoughts. Being careful about what and how we think can open up deeper self-awareness that can, over time, improve our lives.

Perhaps one of the most difficult responsibilities in life is the curating of our thoughts. How we think and what we think is important. We are able to observe and control our bodies, but the mind and its thoughts are not so easily corralled. A simple little thought can cast a shadow over our life before a traffic light turns green. The slightest threat to our ego can overturn our joy and create anger, resentment, and hostility.

We might curate our thoughts in the same way a museum carefully exhibits its treasures. Masterpieces by Rodin, DaVinci, Picasso, and Monet hang in the great hall, but the curator carefully removes the poster advertising a local dog fight. It has no place here. It is violent. It needs to be set aside.

Similarly some of our thoughts need to be discerned and set aside. We need to let go of some attachments, and leave our cell phones turned off. We might replace some of our television time with a good book or a substantive conversation.

And we open our ears and hearts to our failures, tapping on the chalkboard of our lives: "Student, here is how not to do that again. Here is how that happened. Here is what we can learn from that difficult experience." We can learn, but we must give space and time, commiting to a Rule on Thought.

Study Questions for Draft Chapters

Discernment and Discretion

- What would you say in a letter to your future self as an encouragement to making good choices?
- Which is harder for you: saying yes or saying no? Which feels more natural? Why?
- How do consolation (feeling good in your gut about a choice) and desolation (feeling bad in your gut about a choice) play into your decision-making? What role do

you want God to play in that internal work?
- What is your vision for a life of good, careful, and prayerful decision-making?
- What happens when we delude ourselves by choosing things we know are not good moral or ethical choices?

Detachment

- Can you imagine a time when you stop fighting, grabbing, and clutching? What will that life look like?
- What frightens you about the reality that life changes, and things, people, and even our bodies come and go?
- Have you ever experienced equanimity such that something came to you and then left without you anguishing over its loss? These might include a friend, a job, a possession, a home, a way of life, beauty, or health.
- What freedom can you imagine if you greeted all arrivals and departures in your life with serenity, gratefully saying hello to lovely new things and gently saying goodbye to that which life ushers away?
- What would life be like if you could simply let things go when they were taken? How can you coach yourself in that work of spiritual maturity?

Technology and Media

- In what way may you need to confine and channel your relationship with devices?
- What measures might you wish to establish that will invite you to fully enjoy your phones, computers, and tablets while at the same time freeing you from addictions to them?

- Have you ever been without a computer or phone and become agitated and anxious? If yes, then might you have a mild addiction? And if that is the case, what self-imposed rules might help free you to live a "sober" life in which you control your technology and not the reverse?
- How do you feel when someone is talking to you and then starts checking a phone? How might you behave differently?
- What might a chapter on technology do to improve your relationships?
- If we "are what we eat," then what if we "are what we watch" as well? How might this perspective encourage you to rethink and coach yourself on the television programs and movies you allow your eyes to engage?

Study and Formation

- What subjects and writers, thinkers, and leaders do you find inspiring? What books and media do they produce? How would you like these resources to form you?
- How can you make time for study in your daily or weekly routine?
- How do you want to learn from others?
- What books do you want to read this year? (Rewrite this list annually in your Rule and reprint that portion, slipping it back into your book.)

Failure

- When and what have you learned from failures?
- What failures do you see repeating in your life? What might you need to do, learn, study, or get curious about in order to reduce these repetitions?

- What do great thinkers and writers say about failure and how might their thoughts inform yours?
- What is the loving, gentle, kind letter you would write to your future self about a recent failure? How would you encourage yourself?

Closing Prayers

A Prayer for Discernment and Discretion
Mother of knowledge and Father of time, you spoke the planet into creation and so still speak to all of us a "yes" when each morning arrives and nature again asks to exist. So whisper your hopes for us as a mother whispers her hopes for her child: "Live. Grow. Be well. Love deeply and choose well." Give to us your guidance, O God, such that we might know what is right and what is a not-right choice. Remind us gently that you are near and that you have opinions for our lives. And speak those opinions to our consolation and those warnings to our desolation. In the end of days, grant us your peace. Amen.

A Prayer for Detachment
As a baby in your mother's arms, you screamed for milk, for warmth, for cleaning, and for love. So you, Lord Jesus Christ, know that we cling and that we want and that sometimes we need. Speak gently to our cravings—those things we grab and will not let go. Gently help us to release our grip so that we might let go in life's inevitable changes. After three decades of life and love, Jesus, you let go of this life in order to give us ours. You detached from a life lived with beloved friends. Help us to detach from the things to which we so cling— loves, health, possessions, stability, home, status, moments, standards of living—so that when things change as they will, we may loose our own chains and live free of self-made prisons. Amen.

A Prayer for Technology and Media

O Imago Dei, O Image of God, we long for the light of your image and still we wander the Garden of Eden, wanting the tree of knowledge and all its fruit as we seek to be sated. We covet those bright screens, and yet they offer only pseudo-connection and convey the status of overwork. Let us seek your image in each other, in nature, and in prayer and worship so that we do not go to technology for our life-image, our love-images, or wisdom. May we use technology and media as a tool and not as a god. Let there be no other God but you. Free us from this world's silent noisiness. Amen.

A Prayer for Study and Formation

You came to be among us as the Word-made-flesh. You could have come as image or as some other form of god, but you chose to come and be sent as word. Bring to us the Word of God in text and bread and wine. Guide us to writers and speakers whose words bring life. Shield us from words that bring shame or manipulation. Inspire us with your Holy Spirit to be formed and not just educated. So fill us with an awareness of your love that we become Word, like Word, and speak Word to a culture riddled with weak words that obscure truth. Amen.

A Prayer for Failure

Lord Christ, did you ever fail? Surely yes, for you were truly human. And yet you never looked back, only forward. Grant us peace in our failings so that we learn and move on. Help us to break open our egos so that we may learn in the humility of failure and yet stop short of shame. Hold us gently when we know we have done a bad thing, but do not let us ever believe that we are bad people. We and all creation were made, and remain, very good, according to your scriptures. When we succeed, we rejoice, but Lord Christ, limit our pride as a potter confines her spinning clay. When we fail, soothe us with your hands on our souls, massaging them back to hope and openness. Amen.

Chapter 11

On Existence

Two years ago, walking across a street in Prague, I was hit by a speeding city train. I was told I had three hours to live. I remember wondering, half-dazed: What would be on my tombstone? Today, I would be satisfied if the suggested chapter titles of this section were the words engraved on my tombstone: kindness, beauty, the planet, money and philanthropy, and solitude. These words sum up existence for me, and I love writing these chapters since they are a celebration of the life I live.

Our Rule of Life can remind us, coach us, to keep choosing kindness even when life can so easily inspire other, darker ways of living. Our chapter on beauty can remind us to look for it, to make it, to seek it out, and use it to remember God. A chapter on the planet never lets us get too far from the inclination to bend over and touch the grass with a whispered "thank you." Money is a part of every day and you and I need reminders that it is a tool; it is not intrinscially evil—and can do much good. And all these things we can remember in solitude, with a peace that comes from knowing that we are never truly alone. God is with us. Always. We end with this chapter on Existence because it brings us back, in a great circle, to the Listening chapters from which we began.

Chapter Suggestions

Kindness

Am I the only one who needs to sometimes be reminded of kindness? Perhaps. But I doubt it. We all need to be reminded to be kind, gentle, and forgiving, to be congnizant of the great unseen battles being fought inside the people around us.

Let us remember that we cannot see inside the hearts and minds of the people we pass in hallways and street corners. Kindness is different from indifference or neglect. Kindness is an act and even a disposition. It takes effort to be kind. One must overcome fears, regrets, betrayals, and unkindnesses visited upon us and power past them in order to choose kindness. It takes effort and regular reminders to practice this virtue.

What I notice about kindness is that it is a two-handed act. One must put down other things—being right, being sure, being judgmental, being self-righteous. These must be put down in order to pick up kindness. Kindness is like a big box; it takes both hands to hold and requires us to walk gently so as not to trip. I want to be kind. I do not care if I am holy or pious, sinless or blameless, innocent or famous. I don't even care if I am thought of as a particularly good potter or priest or cook. I want to be kind even though I am aware that kindness may not always come my way.

My Rule of Life needs a chapter that reminds me to be kind. When I turn the page of my Rule and see the kindness chapter, I slump in my chair and I remember: "That's right...kindness... that's how I wanted to live...I forgot. Let's do that more."

Beauty

My chapter on beauty reminds me to keep looking for it, to keep seeing it. This chapter reminds me to buy kiwi and carrots for a garnish on a dinner plate. It reminds me to step into the museum and stand in front of my favorite tea bowl— the one in the glass case to the left on the fourth floor with the drip on one side, the one that nearly stops my heart. The chapter reminds me how beautiful my friends are, physically, relationally, spiritually. And it reminds me of the beauty exhibited by my dog Kai, a black Lab with eyes that make me forget my troubles.

At the root of beauty is *eros,* a primordial inner GPS that guides us to what we desire. It is how the species survives: the colors and shapes of bodies, the arousal inside us when we see something we interpret as beautiful.

Celtic theologian John O'Donohue calls this place of desire "the vortex of eros." Life may conceal our desires in busyness or defended solitude, but eros slumbers just below the surface of our tightly buttoned-up selves. Eros is not just sexual; it is a chemical and spiritual response to any beauty. Beauty is a human longing that smolders when it cannot burn and light our lives.

I have a chapter on beauty to remember to look for it, create it, and encourage others to make it. The chapter reminds me also to spend my time with people who love beauty and not with people who are blind to it. Life is short, and the life in which I am in co-creativity with God needs to be lived with people who love beauty.

The Planet

My father was a writer for the aviation and aerospace industry from the 1960s to the 1980s. It was a heady time, and his life was full of spaceships, rockets, astronauts, NASA, and the moon. I remember watching images of Earth and wondering why it was so beautiful in the midst of so many planets of grey rock. It is a privilege to be alive on this blue-green marble.

A chapter in my Rule of Life that considers this planet is the least I can do in response to its stunning beauty. Grass beneath bare feet, morning dew drops, a fawn in the woods, fiddleheads from my New Hampshire farm, a waterfall in the Colorado mountains, a mountainside in Haiti, a desert village in Jordan, monasteries in Russia and in Jerusalem and in Cambridge, a café in Paris, and a diner in Michigan—there are so many lovely plants and places on this planet. I do not want a month to go by when I am not intentionally reminded that this gorgeous, awe-inspiring planet is my home. I want to remember that I am only a caretaker who will hand over this planet to my great-nephew Charlie, who will (hopefully) hand over the planet to his own great-nephew one day. I wonder: What will planet Earth be like then, in 2070, in 2080, in 3000?

My chapter on the planet reminds me to do much more than recycle. It reminds me to use less water, eat more fish and vegetables, use lights in one room at a time, wear sweaters, burn wood fires, light candles, and write checks to agencies that care for animals and land. My chapter on the planet demands that I become an activist.

What are your feelings about this planet? One of the wonderful aspects about writing a Rule of Life is that you get to think about things. You get to think about what you love about this planet, what frightens you, what delights you, what tastes good and feels good. Write a love letter to the planet (and yourself) with thanksgiving for its wonder and beauty. Include a list of the places you want to see and experience. When I read my chapter, I am reminded not to waste vacations. As I visit places, I take them out of the list in my planet chapter and add new places I want to visit, foods I want to eat, and views I want to see before I die.

What do you want to see on this planet before you die? Can you set some goals with a bucket list of places you want to visit and remind yourself of them with this chapter? Can't afford the travel? Well, you might need to add a paragraph to your money chapter (coming next) that challenges you to learn, work, and save. We exist on this amazing planet. What a shame to live on it and not see much of it. You will only be here once. Your chapter on the planet is your chance to challenge yourself.

Money and Philanthropy

My parents were not very good with money. They had enough, but my dad never taught me much about budgeting and saving. I have had to teach myself with books. So I need a chapter in my Rule of Life to encourage me on the subjects of money and philanthropy. Of course, I need money to live, and I also want to embrace philanthropy, which means "lover of humanity." I want to be that kind of person.

My chapter on money reminds me that I want to live within my means. That means I need to live simply, in two rooms. Actually two rooms is more than enough, since I can never occupy both rooms at the same time. I need to regularly use my chapter on money to remember my hopes for financial freedom in old age, and so by reading and re-reading my chapter on money, I remember to save lots and spend little.

In this chapter, I hold myself accountable regarding shopping and possessions. Perhaps you do not have this problem, but I tend to shop for things when I feel powerless. Buying something makes me feel, for a moment, powerful. That is, until the bill shows up. I coach myself in my money chapter by clearly stating the expectation for myself that I will never, ever buy anything on impulse.

When we give money away, the part of our brain that is stimulated by receiving a surprise gift lights up like a Christmas tree. Is that not strange? We humans get pleasure by giving money to others to help them survive. So my chapter reminds me not only to give some of my money away but also to continue the stewardship and fundraising ministry of helping others to do the same. We all help make the planet better by sharing our gifts and talents.

I also set out some very clear goals about debt. Sometimes I meet them, and sometimes I do not. My chapter on money asks me not to carry debt unless it is essential for home or car and even then, to work toward a debt-free life.

My chapter on money reminds me to be careful with it. When this chapter appears in the cycle of my reading, it both annoys me and soothes me. It annoys me because my inner adolescent wants to spend, spend, spend. It soothes me because my inner adult wants a peaceful life.

Solitude

We began our Rule with a set of chapters on listening. We considered silence and stillness as a way toward connection and prayer and as a way to deal with anxious thoughts. In a way, the Rule of Life is like a Zen circle, made with a Japanese brush stroke. We begin, then we proceed around our full set of chapters, and we end back at the beginning. Where does listening end and existence begin? I find it hard to tell sometimes, which is why I have looped the chapters this way.

Some people love solitude, and others hate it. But the reality is that life has some, and in our solitude we face our demons. In facing them, we discover our demons are little more than the man behind the curtain in the *Wizard of Ox*, pulling levers and trying desperately to keep us frightened.

Intentional solitude from time to time is like going into a messy closet, closing the door, and sorting through the clutter. Some things need to be shelved. Some things need to be let go of and placed outside for the trash collection. Some things need to be tried on and smiled at. "What was I thinking when I chose to take this home?" Some things need to be held, cherished, admired, and thanked for giving us so much joy. And then other things in my life I hold in their pieces, broken.

My chapter on solitude asks me to spend time each day alone, sitting and thinking. Sometimes this time is a long period, and on other days, it is short. Of course, the availability of solitude is somewhat dependent on life circumstance. But your Rule of Life offers a chapter on solitude so that you can set a goal for mindfulness. God speaks to us, and we listen, in the solitude into which God meanders. Sometimes we need the silence so we can hear the still, small voice that whispers love, love, love. Our chapters so order our lives that when God does whisper, we hear it. And having heard it, we begin again. We keep going.

There is no such thing as the spiritual life. There is just life. But the spirituality within our lives, seen or unseen, will be found in solitude where the listening begins again and again.

Study Questions for Drafting Chapters

Kindness

- What is your vision for kindness in your life? What longings do you have for a life filled with kindness?
- When do you notice kindness is more likely to emerge from within you? When do you notice kindness in you is crushed? How might you encourage the one and mitigate against the other? Who in your life draws kindness from you? Who crushes it in you?
- What does kindness look like in your life and how might you be kind to yourself?
- What do great thinkers, writers, and scriptures say about kindness and how might some of those quotations inform your chapter on kindness?

Beauty

- Do you want beauty in your life? What kinds of beauty do you want and how might you access that beauty?
- Do you need to renovate your perception of beauty before you can establish your longings for it?
- How does beauty help you to live a better, more authentic, gorgeous life?
- What do you find beautiful? Is that which you find beautiful a part of your life, and if not, how might you get more of it?
- What do you need to add to your life—and set out as goals in this chapter—that will help you enjoy beauty? These might include museums, hikes, travel, reading, audiobooks, friendships, or a chair by a window with a lovely view.

The Planet

- Why does this planet matter to you? What do you love about it?
- Why do you want to take part in caring for the planet? What would that look like?
- How do you want to enjoy the planet? What parts of the planet make you curious and inspire travel?
- What aspects of the planet's loveliness do you like? These might include the blue light of a snowy pre-dawn, sand between your toes, grass underfoot, a mountain stream with rainbow trout, gemstones, lava, smooth snakeskin, heavy cream with vanilla, lavender, watermelon, the eyes of a friend. What does this planet offer you that you want to remember?

Money and Philanthropy

- What kinds of encouragement do you need to give yourself about money?
- Do you have long-term goals that you want to achieve? How can this chapter on money help you achieve those goals?
- What frightens you about money? What do you need to tell yourself in your chapter to allay those fears? What are your hopes and longings for freedom around money?
- What kind of philanthropy do you want to practice in your life?
- What do you need to say about spending, bills, debt, and shopping? What is your vision for a life of freedom around issues of money?

Solitude

- What do you love about solitude? What frightens you about it?
- What can help you to train for solitude in the same way a person trains for running or swimming a race?
- When you are alone with yourself, what happens and how might you coach yourself to create a hospitable setting for solitude? These might include scheduling time, establishing a date night with yourself, creating a space and time to be alone before work or before the family gets up.
- Some people find solitude difficult because they carry shame or guilt. What would it take to let go of these feelings of shame or guilt? What would set you free to enjoy being with yourself?
- Can you imagine a vision for solitude that results in a healthier you? What would that look like and what would need to happen in order to achieve a solitude in which you heal, imagine, and grow curious about new possibilities?
- What do your favorite writers say about solitude? How might they lend you courage to increase solitude and mindfulness in your life?

Next Steps

Kindness, beauty, the planet, money and philanthropy, and solitude all support our most authentic and best selves. Sure, we will, from time to time find ourselves mean, ugly, wasteful, profligate, miserly, and unwilling to see ourselves with solitude's sight. But our chapters in our Rule of Life remind and revision our lives, helping us to remember to be our best selves.

As I consider the titles of chapters in this section, I cannot edit a single one out. I need them all to be a centered, well person. Sure, I could set some lofty new year's resolution to be kind or to be generous, to make time for solitude or even to save electricity, but by February, I will barely recall the January promise, and by March, I will be back to square one. So I write and read daily chapters that keep me on track, bit by bit, day by day, reminder by reminder, and step by step.

It works. It has for monks and nuns for centuries. So why not take this life-technology by the hand from the cloister and lead it through the garden and through the tall-walled gate, into the street and down the lane and into our own kitchen?

It is time for a Rule of Life to move from the cloister to the kitchen. It is time for the rest of us to use this amazing technology of living a well life. It is time to stop peeking over the cloister wall into the peaceable kingdom that they have created. It is time to make our homes, our neighborhoods, our nation, and our world into that peaceable kingdom, one person, one Rule, one chapter, one page turn at a time.

Closing Collects

A Prayer for Kindness
Kind, you were so often, Lord Christ, as you wandered the earth touching the sick and holding children up to see them eye to eye. Make kindness my goal and my work. When I am hard, soften me. When I am sharp, dull my edges. Replace my piety with gentleness. Help me to be kind to myself and graciously extend that kindness to others. Amen.

A Prayer for Beauty
When our scriptures call you the Good Shepherd, they do not do the Hebrew justice. You are the beautiful shepherd. You made all of creation beautiful. Help me to see beauty when ugly fills my heart. Let anger, fear, resentment, and hatred be transfigured by the beauty all around me. Amen.

A Prayer for the Planet
Set at the perfect distance from the sun and tilted on the perfect axis for light and dark, water and ice, you have placed this planet to host life. Without the planet placed just so, water would not freeze, and soil would not host vegetation. Sand would not warm, wind and water would not gather for life's Leviathans. Thank you. That is all one can say when walking on grass and eating candied ginger. Thank you for this planet. So guide our lives that we might share its bounty with all of humanity and so guide our loves that we pass it on to future generations with integrity. Amen.

A Prayer for Money and Philanthropy
We live in systems that employ the use of money, as did you, Christ Jesus. The women who followed you raised the money you needed for food and lodging as you and your friends walked the Way. So fill us with your love that we use money carefully, living simply so that others may simply live. When we are reckless, call us to center. When we have more than we need, inspire generosity. You love, you create, and you give yourself away. Gently guide us into our Imago Dei, our imagining of your divine three-fold nature. Amen.

A Prayer for Solitude

Up into the mountains you went to be alone. What did you do there? You listened; you looked inside yourself. You recollected the day before and imagined the day to come. You thought about life and love, about your friends and your calling. Give us the grace to sit alone in solitude with the time to consider our lives, the courage to consider our callings, and the wisdom to consider our choices. Help us to curate a life of deep intention and not of reckless speed. Let us see ourselves that we might see you there, eyes wide and smiling love into the darkest recesses of our souls, so that we may become a light to the world and a lamp to the love you kindle through us, the body of Christ. Amen.

Afterword

A Rule of Life helps us to make good, daily choices, to be converted into the people we want to become. It is a life-core curriculum that can release us from forgetfulness and apathy, reconnecting us to our own true selves.

A few chapters in my Rule are there for use in emergencies—like those wall boxes that say: "In an emergency, break glass and use." These chapters include tragedy, failure, grief, and loss.

If you are like me (and most people), you will start writing your Rule with great enthusiasm and then hit a writer's block or two before completion. I encourage you to push through these times. They will come, but they will also go.

You will probably also find that, at times, you read your chapters daily and faithfully but then skip them, in the same way that we sometimes skip daily exercise routines in periods of resistance. The thing to do is to "fake it 'til you make it." Get back to it, and you will slowly re-warm to its routines.

When the Going Gets Tough

It is one thing to want a Rule of Life. It is quite another to actually write one. But you can do it! You have already made a great first step with reading this book. Most people don't even recognize that their lives have drifted into a cycle of not living their dream. Indeed most people have not even considered that a dream is possible, let alone discerned one. You have summoned a lot of courage just to get this far. Congratulations.

For some, writing will come naturally. For others, it will be difficult. What is important is to be gentle with yourself.

When I first wrote my Rule of Life, I established a schedule to make the process more manageable. Here is a guideline to help you establish a timeline for writing your Rule.

Week One
Draft a list of chapters.
If you are going to write thirty chapters (30 sets of 300-600 words), draft a list of 40 or 50 topics. Take some time to consider the different areas, then edit the list down to the thirty you want.

Week Two
Think about content for the chapters.
I carry around index cards, one for each chapter. You might prefer to make notes on your iPhone. Label each card (or file) with a potential chapter title, and then jot things down as they come to you.

Weeks Three-Ten
Write the chapters from the index cards or notes.
Try writing a few chapters on the subjects you know pretty well. Don't worry about how polished they are. This is a

lifetime document, so the first draft might take some time
to write. Then start on chapters that are tougher to write.
Make sure to give yourself at least one sabbath day off from
writing each week.

If you face writer's block, let the work rest for a day or two
but do not go more than three days or you run the risk of
not getting back to it. Do not let that happen.

Mark out time in your calendar for writing and then log
the chapters you completed each day (or week) so you can
look back with some satisfaction on the work you have
accomplished.

The Daily Read and Recollection

Once you have finished your Rule of Life, it is time to start
reading. Each day, read one chapter. Try not to skip ahead
or move around the order. You will be amazed at how often
your chapter will speak to you about an issue you are facing.
When you finish the thirty days, return to the beginning and
start anew.

From time to time you may not want to read your Rule.
This resistance is normal and often shows up when you are
also resisting prayer, intimacy with a partner, exercise, and
other life choices. What I find works is simply to read the
Rule regardless of whether I want to or not. Sometimes we
must simply show up even if we are just going through the
motions. You might want to write a chapter in your Rule that
encourages you to remember why you wanted a Rule in the
first place.

It takes sixty-six days to form a new habit so keep reading your
chapters and mark your calendar for about two and a half

months. In two cycles of thirty chapters, you will be well on your way to making this a life tool.

And now, gentle reader, this is up to you. Getting started and moving forward, with a daily or weekly goal for writing, will get your Rule written. Only you can write this document to channel your passions, guide your choices, and form your soul.

Perhaps there are people whose lives would not be improved with a daily reminder of their hopes for a good, guided life. Personally, I do not know any.

Our little notes to self plug us into God's grace the way medicine moves us from illness into health. They are a gift from yourself to yourself, and God's voice is within them.

APPENDIX

Sample Chapters

These sample chapters are from the author's own Rule of Life.

A Chapter on Creativity

Dear Charles,

You are made in God's image and are made therefore to reflect God's essential existence as creator, lover, and giver—live that image and you will live authentically. Just as a child has his father's nose or mother's cheek line, we have God's creativity. There is no such thing as an uncreative person. There is only a creative person whose circumstance or limiting beliefs are barriers to creativity. And so, Charles, create.

Work addiction, worry, laziness, boredom, anger, and grief will erode the creativity that you want to foster in your life. Try hard to be aware when one of these spiritual illnesses creeps into your life, curdling creativity. In your recollection at the end of each day, as you prepare for sleep, try to remember those things you have created—things let loose into the day and onto the planet—hoping with great hope that what you have created was good, honest, beautiful, and kind. If you have created anything of which you are ashamed, such as perpetuating a rumor or creating an unkind comment, try to take time to notice it with God's eye, ask forgiveness, and make immediate amends.

You are a potter, though your work addiction is a constant threat to that beautiful way of being. So work hard to carve out time each week for throwing pots, glazing or firing, especially simple tea bowls. Make time to write. And create hospitality for friends and for friendships' gestation. Let those who neglect it or reject it or betray it do so. Just keep going.

Your friends who like to create will be a source of great joy for you and so hold creativity high on the list of the attributes of your friends. We will make pots and meals, conversations and beauty, and even occasionally host our grief together.

At times, you will write and pray in silence, and that too will be a creative time. If you are not writing, making pots, singing robustly, or cooking, then notice that absence and wonder what grief or fear you hold. Seek help to find the source of the grief or loss that is blocking your creativity. Try to create ways to offer love, no matter what you receive in return.

A Chapter on Work

Dear Charles,

Let your work be good, kind, effective, and also contained. You are, sweet one, an addict. Sorry, but it's true. Your addiction of choice is work. Your addiction will always be encouraged and even rewarded in the church and in this ill society—so be extra careful and mindful.

You anesthetize your pain with work and, furthermore, you live in a society whose addiction to work and to its resulting income is pathological, making awareness all the more important. You must live differently, or you will be able to help nobody. You do overwork, sweet self-friend, terribly. You know you do. Your overwork then fosters male passivity and its resulting rage. Stay in connection to your sponsor and go to the meetings.

Work, like alcohol, food, and shopping, can be wonderful in and of itself but also a threat to your wellness if you lose your balance. You will occasionally be jealous of those whose lives do not seem to struggle with addictions. Do not use work to anesthetize your pain in life. Face the pain, Charles. Feel the pain. Let it show you and teach you. When work addiction unfurls like a beautiful dragon, try to notice its camouflage—be mindful, always aware and awake. You, sweet one, have been liberated by God from the slaveries of the various forms of Egypt in your life, so let this chapter remind you that you will not work as a modern American economy-slave, even for money, possessions, position, or prestige.

Pottery, cooking for friends, writing, preaching, teaching, gardening, beekeeping, reading, massage, soul conversations —this work you love—makes you your best self and can be both an expression of your potency and charism. And yet, you are a mere mortal—one who needs rest during a day, a week, a month, and a year. So, take your rest and let your close friends remind you to be kind to yourself, for so often you are not kind to yourself.

You must spend extra time in discernment and discretion when it comes to your yes and your no when invitations for work arrive. You are worthy of love without working to earn it. You have a tendency to get your self-esteem from the work you do.

You need not. Work is not your source of self-esteem. You are beautiful, flawed, and human, but your work is not the way to get attention or approval. Your calendar will be important to your success around the boundaries of work. Schedule work carefully, but also schedule periods of play, friendship, and rest—even solitude. If you are not careful, work will consume you, even kill you. Your addiction will rob you of your life. Be awake to this. God loves you. You are beloved and enough.

A Chapter on Money

Dear Charles,

Your heart tells you that all shall be well, that everything you have comes from God and that you have enough. The media tells you that your money is a way to get what you want, that you do not have enough and that your status is seen by your style of life. The media is wrong and yet you will spend a lot of time with its many forms. You will need to be resilient in remembering who you are.

You have been raised by people whose attachment to money was not healthy, and so you will need to seek healing in the area of money. Occasionally you will attempt to soothe hurt feelings, insecurities, loneliness, or boredom by spending money both in an effort to get a hit of power and control and as a means to purchase things that give you a momentary sense of satisfaction. Think, dear one, for a moment now, of the many things you have bought and then lost, discarded, given away, or stored in closets and garages. Please Charles, live simply, free of too many possessions, too many rooms, and too much of a car.

Remember to live within your means on a weekly basis, never misusing credit by purchasing unessential things for which you do not have the funds available in your budget. Never, ever spend money spontaneously on something you were not seeking. Please do not make impulse purchases—ever. Wait twenty-four hours before buying something you see on television, the internet, or even wandering in a store. Do not shop recreationally. Ask yourself to feel the poverty of having to say no to yourself when you want something you cannot afford or do not need. Live by a budget, checking your progress regularly so as not to over-spend. Be attentive to turning off lights, taking care with food leftovers, lowering heat and air conditioning, and using firewood so as not to waste what God has given to you and our planet. Live on half of your salary, if you can.

Be grateful for what you have. When you wake, before getting out of bed, and at night when you lay down before you sleep, list in prayer what you have been given and be grateful. Your gifts to your retirement, to your church, and to charities will always be your first checks written each month. And when you wish you had more than you do, try to remember how much you do have and squeeze out a prayer of gratitude as an antidote to envy or despair.

Create walls of defense in your Rule of Life against a society, its media, and its changing church, all with deep pathology about money. Live joyfully on little and when they sneer at your car, your possessions, your address or clothes, remember yourself and your longing for simplicity in the way of Jesus.

A Chapter on Kindness

Dear Charles,

You know with what joyful ferocity you hold kindness to be a virtue in others, so keep it a virtue in yourself. Before you speak, always ask yourself: "Is it kind? Is it true? Does it improve on the silence?" Make kindness a priority; however, become nobody's fool.

Says George Sand, "Guard well within yourself that treasure, kindness. Know how to give without hesitation, how to lose without regret, how to acquire without meanness." Remember that kindness is your treasure: not money, not prestige, not possessions, and not power. And yet, people will give you power when you are kind to them, so curate it wisely and with great care, the way you would hold a butterfly or a six-tiered buttercream wedding cake on a summer's day. Or even nitroglycerin. Carefully.

Notice what encourages kindness in you and what harms or blocks it. Charles, you are less kind when isolated, on too much caffeine, when you overwork or get overtired, and when you have not processed betrayal, pain, or anger carefully. Live a well-life so that kindness has a chance at incubation. Kindness is like yeast, powerful and fragile. Let kindness be a bellwether for friendships, and the lack of it, your canary in the mineshafts of your life. If you see a lack of kindness in a friend, do not try to judge, change, or label them. Simply step away. There will be other friends to come along. Curate your friendships daily. Look to the ways Jesus was kind and to whom Jesus was kind.

For better or worse, you are a priest. The priesthood is your calling, and yet it has been a difficult burden. Some congregants, clergy, and bishops have been loving, honest, kind, encouraging, present, and effective. Others have been unkind, lazy, incompetent, creepy, or manipulative. Be kind, but do not be naive, gullible, or used. You can be kind without giving up your power or your potency.

Remember the words of encouragement from Nelson Mandela: "A good head and good heart are always a formidable combination. But when you add to that a literate tongue or pen, then you have something very special." So write, yes my friend, write with fervor. But write kindly, remembering that you have no idea what others have suffered, are suffering, or will suffer. So make your smile and your words kind no matter what others do to you. And when you can't be kind, at least be quiet and even solitary until you can, again, be kind.

Rule of Life
for Groups

Groups can write a Rule of Life too, depending on the needs of the group, and how often they meet.

When I was visiting inmates in a prison near Charlottesville, Virginia, I found myself meeting weekly with a man named Joe. He was in prison for murder and lived in a cell block with seven other inmates, each of whom had a bunk. Every week, Joe and I would talk about his writing a Rule of Life so that he could self-coach his life choices in a new way. He was an amazing student, writing thoughtfully and creatively. And we would often discuss what could be cut to get his chapters down to six hundred words or so.

The other inmates pretended to read books, nap, and watch TV. But in fact, they were listening. One day they asked if the eight of them could write a group Rule of Life that would help them live together more effectively. Joe would read his own chapter alone and then share a chapter each day with the other inmates, who wrote their own. The group of men in that group cell, I am told, became close friends and were remarkably well-centered and happy.

A Rule for a Vestry or Board

A church vestry or a religious board of directors might want just ten chapters for a Rule of Life. This number might match their ten yearly meetings, helping the group remember who and how it wants to be as a community of Christian practice.

Some possible chapter titles include:

- Prayer
- Community
- Discernment
- Discretion
- Conversation
- Conflict
- Unity in diversity
- Leadership
- Christ-likeness
- Spiritual practice

Each of these titles could be worked into a short chapter to be read at the beginning or end of a vestry meeting. These chapters might help form the life, longings, and integrity of the group, contributing to its health and mitigating against dysfunctions.

A Rule for a Couple

A married couple might wish to use a Rule of Life to discern, then establish what they long for in marriage or for their family. This series of a dozen or two dozen statements, when read aloud by a couple in their private work on their marriage can provide a safe container for needful conversations.

I know of couples who use their Rule of Life when going
to bed at night. They talk about their day—its successes, its
failures—and then, before a brief prayer, they turn the page of
the Rule they have written and read the three hundred or more
words.

The chapters particular to a marriage might include:

- Honesty
- Forgiveness
- Anger
- Conversation
- Intimacy
- Touch
- Kindness
- Rest
- Date night
- Betrayals
- Unity
- Decisions
- Church
- Health
- Conflict
- Friendship
- Attractions
- Finances
- Aging
- Sickness
- Travel
- Prayer
- Mutual delight
- Families
- Sabbath-keeping
- Space
- Sex
- Mutual support
- Children (or chapters for each child)
- Holidays

A Rule for a Family

I know two families who have written a Rule of Life with their children and read it together at the breakfast table. In fact, having breakfast together is one of the main and early chapters. This gives them a time to check in and be a family together, especially important given how often evenings are disrupted by soccer practice and meetings, sleepovers and television. Each morning they sit with the binder in the center of the table and turn the page to the next new chapter of their Rule of Life, taking turns reading it aloud. Each chapter is short because the children are young. And the chapters are rewritten every few years as the children grow.

One friend uses a Rule with his family that includes these titles:
- Family night
- Truth
- Rest
- Playfulness
- Supporting each other
- Privacy, not secrets
- Generosity
- Loving kindness
- When we hurt each other
- Forgiveness
- Awareness
- Sharing

Resources

Rule of Life and Monastic Life

- *The Monastic Rules* by Augustine of Hippo (New City Press, 2003)

- *The Zen Monastic Experience: Buddhist Practice in Contemporary Korea* by Robert E. Buswell Jr. (Princeton University Press, 1992)

- *The Way of Simplicity: The Cisterian Tradition* by Esther De Waal (Orbis Books, 1998)

- *Monk Habits for Everyday People: Benedictine Spirituality for Protestants* by Dennis Okholm (Brazos Press, 2007)

- *Freedom Wherever We Go: A Buddhist Monastic Code for the Twenty-first Century* by Thich Nhat Hanh (Parallax Press, 2004)

- *Regular Life: Monastic, Canonical and Mendicant Rules* by Daniel Marcel la Corte and Douglas J. McMillan (Medieval Institute Publications, 2004)

- *Gifts of the Desert: The Forgotten Path of Christian Spirituality* by Kyriacoa C. Markides (Random House, Inc., 2007)

- *Present over Perfect: Leaving Behind Frantic for a Simpler, More Soulful Way of Living* by Shauna Niequist (Zondervan, 2016)
- *The Cloister Walk* by Kathleen Norris (Riverhead Books, 1996)
- *The Artist's Rule: Nurturing Your Creative Soul with Monastic Wisdom* by Christine Valters Paintner (Sorin Books, 2011)
- *The Urban Monk: Eastern Wisdom and Modern Hacks to Stop Time and Find Success, Happiness, and Peace* by Pedram Shojai (Rodale, 2016)
- *The Rule of the Society of Saint John The Evangelist* (Cowley Publications, 1997)
- *A Monk in the World* by Wayne Teasdale (New World Library, 2010)
- *The Rules of Life* by Richard Templar (Prentice Hall, 2006)
- *Beyond the Walls: Monastic Wisdom for Everyday Life* by Paul Wilkes (Doubleday, 1999)

Life Skills and Spirituality

- *Rising Strong: How the Ability to Reset Transforms the Way We Live, Love, Parent, and Lead* by Brené Brown, (Penguin Random House, 2015)
- *Loving What Is: Four Questions That Can Change Your Life* by Byron Katie, (Harmony Books, 2002)
- *Longing and Belonging: The Complete John O'Donohue Audio Collection* by John O'Donohue (Amazon, 2013)
- *Centering in Pottery, Poetry, and the Person* by M.C. Richards (Wesleyan University Press, 1989)

- *Personality Types: Using the Enneagram for Self-Discovery* by Don Richard Riso and Russ Hudso (Houghton Mifflin Harcourt, 1996)
- *The Fire of Your Life* by Maggie Ross (Seabury Books, 2007)
- *Pillars of Flame: Power, Priesthood, and Spiritual Maturity* by Maggie Ross (Church Publishing, Inc., 2007)
- *Silence: A User's Guide* by Maggie Ross (Darton, Longman & Todd, 2014)
- *Becoming Wise* by Krista Tippet (Penguin Press, 2016)

Prayer and Meditation

- *The Art of Stillness: Adventures in Going Nowhere* by Pico Iyer (Simon & Schuster/TED, 2014)
- *Wherever You Go, There You Are: Mindfulness Meditation In Everyday Life* by Jon Kabat-Zinn (Hatchette Books, 2010)
- *Full Catastrophe Living: Using the Wisdom of Your Body & Mind to Face Stress, Pain & Illness* by Jon Kabat-Zinn (Random House, Inc.,1990)
- *Listening for the Heartbeat of God: A Celtic Spirituality* by John Philip Newell (Paulist Press, 1997)

Writing

- *Writing Tools: 55 Essential Strategies for Every Writer* by Roy Peter Clark (Little, Brown and Company, 2008)
- *Big Magic: Creative Living Beyond Fear* by Elizabeth Gilbert (Riverhead Books, 2015)

- *Writing to Wake the Soul: Opening the Sacred Conversation Within* by Karen Hering (Atria Books, 2013)
- *Echoing Silence: Thomas Merton on the Vocation of Writing* by Robert Inchausti (New Seeds Books, 2007)
- *Writing as a Sacred Path: A Practical Guide to Writing with Passion and Purpose* by Jill Jepson (Celestial Arts, 2008)
- *The Art of Memoir* by Mary Karr (HarperCollins Publishers, 2015)
- *On Writing: A Memoir Of The Craft* by Stephen King (Scribner, 2000)
- *Word by Word* by Anne Lamott (Anchor Books, 1995)
- *Bird by Bird* by Anne Lamott (Anchor Books, 1994)
- *Writing To Heal: A Guided Journal for Recovering from Trauma and Emotional Upheaval* by James W. Pennebaker (New Harbinger Publications, 2004)

Chapters

Addiction
- *In the Realm of Hungry Ghosts: Close Encounters with Addiction* by Gabor Mate (North Atlantic Books, 2010)

Aging
- *Falling Upward: A Spirituality for the Two Halves of Life* by Richard Rohr (Jossey-Bass, 2011)

Anger
- *Anger* by Thich Nhat Hanh (Riverhead Books, 2001)

Difficult times
- *When Things Fall Apart: Heart Advice for Difficult Times* by Pema Chödrön (Shambhala, 2000)

Discernment
- *Discernment: Reading the Signs of Daily Life* by Henri Nouwen (HarperCollins, 2013)

Fear
- *The Places that Scare You: A Guide to Fearlessness in Difficult Times* by Pema Chödrön (Shambhala, 2002)
- *The Science of Fear: How the Culture of Fear Manipulates Your Brain* by Daniel Gardner (Dutton Adult, 2008)

Friendship
- *The Politics of Friendship* by Jacques Derrida, translated by George Collins (Verso, 1997)
- *Anam Cara: A Book of Celtic Wisdom* by John O'Donohue (HarperCollins Publishers, 1997)

Focus
- *The One Thing: The Surprisingly Simple Truth Behind Extraordinary Results* by Gary Keller and Jay Papasan (Bard Press, 2012)

Goodness
- *Made for Goodness: And Why This Makes All the Difference* by Desmond Tutu and Mpho Tutu (HarperCollins Publishers, 2010)

Silence

- *A Book of Silence* by Sara Maitland (Counterpoint Press, 2008)
- *Writing the Icon of the Heart: In Silence Beholding* by Maggie Ross (Cascade Books, 2013)

Simplicity

- *The Complete Idiot's Guide to Simple Living* by Georgene Lockwood (Alpha Books, 2000)
- *The Not So Big Life: Making Room for What Really Matters* by Sarah Susanka (Random House, 2007)

Sin

- *Disordered Loves: Healing the Seven Deadly Sins* by William S. Stafford (Cowley Publications, 1994)
- *Joy in Confession: Reclaiming Sacramental Reconciliation* by Hillary D. Raining (Forward Movement, 2017)

Slowing Down

- *In Praise of Slowness: Challenging the Cult of Speed* by Carl Honore (HarperCollins Publishers, 2004)

Stuck Places

- *Acedia & me: A Marriage, Monks, and a Writer's Life* by Kathleen Norris (Riverhead Books, 2008)

Uncertainty

- *Comfortable with Uncertainty: 108 Teachings on Cultivating Fearlessness and Compassion* by Pema Chödrön (Shambhala, 2003)

About the Author

Since his conversion at the age of nine, alone in a church sanctuary while on a mission to get a Cub Scout religion badge, Charles LaFond has loved Jesus and has tried hard, often successfully, to love the Body of Christ we call the church. Raised in Montreal, Charles sensed a call to the priesthood and to test a monastic vocation in his early teens.

Educated at The University of the South in French literature simply because it was beautiful, Charles graduated to become a missionary in Haiti weeks after the Duvalier family fled, sending the nation into a series of terrible years. After a year in Haiti, Charles entered a career in financial development, working at the College of William and Mary and then as vice president of the YMCA of Greater Richmond. He then went to seminary at Virginia Theological Seminary. After a curacy in Charlottesville where he lived on Monticello's estate, Charles moved to Cambridge, Massachusetts, where he tested a vocation at the Society of Saint John The Evangelist in a three-year novitiate. Ultimately, he chose not to take vows but rather to purchase a farm in New Hampshire from which he traveled the Episcopal Diocese of New Hampshire as canon for congregational life and served as chaplain to the New Hampshire State Senate.

Maintaining his nineteenth-century farm and pottery studio in New Hampshire's White Mountain foothills, Charles wrote this book in summers there and also while serving full-time at the Episcopal Cathedral of Saint John's in the Wilderness in Denver, Colorado. As canon steward at the cathedral, he served the congregation as pastor and teacher and raised annual and capital resources for mission. Author of two previous books, *Fearless Church Fundraising* and *Fearless Major Gifts: Inspiring Meaning-making*, Charles is a weekly contributor to Episcopal Café for "The Daily Sip" and the Fearless Fundraising blog series.

An Episcopal priest, teacher, retreat leader and writer, Charles and his companion, Kai, now live on a twenty-acre horse farm raising apples and peaches, where they read his Rule of Life most days. They are members of an area house-church based around silent prayer, study, spiritual practice, and very fine soups and fresh breads. Charles now raises money to house those experiencing homelessness. He is a master potter (www.charleslafond.net) and maintains a private studio called Setting Moon Pottery at Coyote Clay Studios in downtown Albuquerque.

About Forward Movement

Forward Movement inspires disciples and empowers evangelists. Our mission is to support you in your spiritual journey and to help you grow as a follower of Jesus Christ. We live out our ministry by publishing books, daily reflections, studies for small groups, and online resources.

Forward Day by Day is read daily by Christians around the world and is also available in Spanish (*Adelante Día a Día*) and Braille, online, as a podcast, and as an app for your smartphones or tablets. We donate nearly 30,000 copies each quarter to prisons, hospitals, and nursing homes. We actively seek partners across the church and look for ways to provide resources that inspire and challenge.

A ministry of the Episcopal Church for eighty years, Forward Movement is a nonprofit organization funded by sales of resources and gifts from generous donors.

To learn more about Forward Movement and its resources, please visit www.ForwardMovement.org. We are delighted to be doing this work and invite your prayers and support.